LEGACY OF LOVE

LEGACY OF LOVE
DENNIS A. McINTYRE

Tate Publishing & *Enterprises*

Legacy of Love
Copyright © 2008 by Dennis A. McIntyre. All rights reserved.

This title is also available as a Tate Out Loud product. Visit www.tatepublishing.com for more information.

No part of this publication may be reproduced, stored in a retrieval system or transmitted in any way by any means, electronic, mechanical, photocopy, recording or otherwise without the prior permission of the author except as provided by USA copyright law.

Scripture quotations marked "NIV" are taken from the *Holy Bible, New International Version* ®, Copyright © 1973, 1978, 1984 by International Bible Society. Used by permission of Zondervan Publishing House. All rights reserved.

The opinions expressed by the author are not necessarily those of Tate Publishing, LLC.

Published by Tate Publishing & Enterprises, LLC
127 E. Trade Center Terrace | Mustang, Oklahoma 73064 USA
1.888.361.9473 | www.tatepublishing.com

Tate Publishing is committed to excellence in the publishing industry. The company reflects the philosophy established by the founders, based on Psalm 68:11,
"The Lord gave the word and great was the company of those who published it."

Book design copyright © 2008 by Tate Publishing, LLC. All rights reserved.
Cover design by Lynly D. Taylor
Interior design by Joey Garrett

Published in the United States of America
ISBN: 978-1-60696-116-2
1. Biography & Autobiography: Personal Memoirs
08.08.18

DEDICATION

Legacies are all we can leave on earth after we leave this world. Worldly possessions may be treasured for a brief time, but a legacy built on love can last for generations. Most of us cannot remember who won the World Series two years ago, yet we can recall people who touched our lives generations ago. This book is the story of a man who was far from rich but left a priceless legacy of love. He was my dad.

As a soldier in World War II, Dad demonstrated courage and dedication to his country and comrades with two purple hearts as mementos. The loss of his wife left him financially bankrupt and tasked with the challenge of raising three boys alone. She was the wage earner and Dad stayed at home as a caretaker. His dreams were replaced with the hope that somehow his children would stay together and he would be able to support his family. Dad's perseverance, dedication and love were his legacy. Three young boys have since grown and raised families of their own. The values our father demonstrated have been passed on. In a world where divorce and broken commitments approach normalcy, faithfulness and love have taken root in our families. Trials are a certainty of life. Dad taught us how to deal with them.

After losing a second wife, Dad took the time to write down significant facts about our mother for all of his children to know. He wrote them on three separate index cards, placed them behind enlarged photos of our mother, and presented them to each son. That gift of love triggered several conversations, which led to the details shared in this book. Mom's picture reminds me of my heritage. The index card reminds me that I am a child of loving parents.

Originally, this manuscript was written for family members so that my father's legacy would continue for generations to follow. God had a different plan that would involve my wife of nearly thirty-eight years. Dottie was a faithful servant, who let the light of Jesus shine on everyone she met. She was an inspiration to her family, her friends, and anyone who had the privilege to know her. Her battle with cancer demonstrated courage and the joy she felt knowing that God was right there with her. Her spirit was infectious on others going through similar difficulties. Her legacy of love lives on in this book as well.

I dedicate this book to my wife, my father, and my Savior, Christ Jesus.

PREFACE

Many books have been written, depicting the tragedies of life. In the film industry, tragic events have been mixed with stories of love and hope, while the event still remains tragic. The *Titanic* still sank with hundreds of lives being lost. The loss of a loved one can affect generations to follow, when it happens unexpectedly. My life had such an event as my mother was taken away by cancer when I was three years of age. Events began to unfold as a result of her loss that impacted my brothers, my father, and myself.

This manuscript serves to be a legacy to my family, my brothers' families, and others who have shaped the lives of my brothers and I. It is not a story about pain and sorrow, although these elements are portrayed. Rather it is a legacy of love, that I feel needs to be shared. It is the story of three boys who face life with several tests of character. It is the story of a father whose heart becomes bitter and resentful to his Creator, and yet struggles to keep his sons close. It is a testimony for others, who are facing similar hardships, to receive strength and hope to face the future.

It is my deepest desire to share a message of love, hope, and joy to those who mourn. We are not alone as we pass through this world. It took me about fifty years to come to grips with the things that have held my emotions in turmoil. The Bible tells us in

1Corinthians 13: 11–13 (NIV):

> When I was a child, I talked like a child, I thought like a child, I reasoned like a child. When I became a man, I put childish ways behind me. Now we see but a poor reflection as in a mirror; then we shall see face to face. Now I know in part; then I shall know fully, even as I am known. And now these three remain: faith, hope, and love. But the greatest of these is love.

The reflection that I have seen is still cloudy, but I believe I have been blessed with a few insights into the very heart of God, full of love, compassion, and ultimate joy. It cannot be adequately expressed in words, but was felt when the scales of bitterness fell from my dad's countenance and written on the faces of my grandchildren.

TABLE OF CONTENTS

- 11   Psalm 23 (NIV)
- 13   About Dad
- 19   About Mom
- 23   Then They Were Five
- 27   Why Did You Have to Go, Mom?
- 33   A Family Again
- 39   Three Different Brothers
- 47   A New Dream Begins
- 53   The Dream Becomes Reality

59	Then There Were Four
69	A Spiritual Realization
75	Rumbling Emotions
81	Keeping Commitments
91	The Reunion
97	A New Battle
107	God's Calling
123	Lessons To Be Learned
127	Emotions of a Child
133	Effects on Brothers
143	Power of Prayer
147	Conclusion

PSALM 23 (NIV)

The Lord is my shepherd, I shall not want.
He makes me lie down in green pastures,
He leads me besides still waters,
He restores my soul.
He guides me in paths of righteousness for his name's sake.
Even though I walk through the valley of the shadow of death,
I will fear no evil, for you are with me.
You prepare a table before me in the presence of my enemies.
You anoint my head with oil; my cup overflows.
Surely goodness and love will follow me all the days of my life,
And I will dwell in the house of the Lord forever.

ABOUT DAD

History books speak volumes about the events of World War II and the sacrifices made to preserve a peaceful world. Millions of people were being slaughtered because they were born Jewish. The world watched as Adolph Hitler methodically convinced his people that their lower standard of living was directly due to the prosperity of the Jews. America had heard and seen enough. Our allies united and declared war to end the tyranny. My dad, LaVerne McIntyre, was drafted around the age of thirty and sent to the battlefront.

He was the middle of three sons along with a sister. When LaVerne was a teenager, his father passed away. His mother, Verna, made meals from the vegetation on the farm, as the family income was minimal. Perhaps the name LaVerne was chosen as the male counterpart to his mother's name. Throughout the years his mother would call dad "Verne."

His military comrades and friends would affectionately call him "Mac." Meat was a luxury and yet love was shared. Dad did what he could to work the farm and dropped out of school after completing the sixth grade. Now he was being called to war. The thoughts that must have gone through his mind were probably focused on who would help his mother with the work that needed to be done. Perhaps he thought about helping by sending a portion of the small wages he would make as a soldier. Nevertheless, he did not shrug his military duties. His country needed him.

Being needed by someone is an amazing thing for humans to understand. There is something powerful that occurs when someone approaches each of us and said *I need you.* These words give us a sense of purpose when we may be struggling with identifying who we are. Uncle Sam said, I need you, and perhaps Dad understood that to mean far more. His life at thirty may have caused him to rethink where he had been. Perhaps, he now became focused on where he was heading. The thought of preparing for war was a far cry from that of planting, hoeing, and picking crops. Holding a gun and killing the enemy was far removed from pitching horseshoes with friends. His new friends would now be on the battlefront. Many of them would die before he returned home.

The United States Army called and away he went. He was there at Normandy as he saw firsthand many lives lost. Those whom he only knew for a few weeks were gone as quickly as they hit the beach. It was more than a new experience. It was a living hell. Each day may have begun with the thought that it might be the last for many of the soldiers. Each night ended with thought of home and family. As letters were distributed to the men of his platoon, I can picture the look of hope on my dad's face. Each letter was a treasure to be sure. Later, Dad and I would talk about how he would save every one and reread them over and over. He started collecting the stamps as a way of coping. Other comrades would support his newfound hobby and give him their stamps. Foxholes were not so lonely when a piece of home was there as well.

A soldier once made the statement, "There are no atheists in foxholes." I have tried to imagine what my father must have thought about so far away from home in the midst of a bloody war. Each day could have been his last. The letters from home must have sustained him to some degree, but the thought of death may have had an even deeper impact on his soul. Somehow I picture a man who was taught spiritual values as a boy from his parents and reached deep into his memories to recall a hymn or a prayer. The twenty-third Psalms may well have gripped his heart in the heat of battle. The "valley of the shadow of death" certainly was a description of the foxholes of war. Dad was not an atheist and if he had a Bible in his possessions, I can see him reading it when the opportunity to do so rose.

The emotions of a soldier in battle may have been trained to take a step back, where they interfered with the commitment to the cause. The spiritual side may have been on the front line. Perhaps Dad was spared during that time because of the prayers of his family and friends. Believing that you are not alone is a powerful sustaining force as well. To believe that an all powerful and loving God can be with us during the most treacherous moments of our existence carries another level of peace. Perhaps Dad was spared because of that kind of relationship and God was answering his prayers throughout the conflict. These are merely suggestions on my part, but my father did have faith in a Creator. It may not have been the kind to move mountains, but it was there, as I will share about it later in this account.

Dad had one sustaining person with him in thought in the foxholes of WWII. Her name was Rae Wyland. He dated her as a college student near his hometown in New York State and would receive correspondence from her across the ocean. At times Rae would send her picture, which would be a source or strength, hope, and pride. His foxhole friends would have to listen to that pride. To Dad, her picture would easily rival a Bette Gable pin-up. When the war opened up times of relief, her pictures and letters would serve to console him. His heart would grow fonder with each day. I am sure that his first desire when he returned from war was to be with her. It would be a sustaining thought during the agony around him.

In the years while my dad served his country, he learned many things about life. He understood what it meant to have the support from his family. He knew that lives were on the line if he did not do as he was commanded. Therefore, his word was his bond. He learned a lot about dying, respect, honor, pride, and courage. He learned how to make the most of seemingly bad situations. With two Purple Hearts from wounds in his left arm and left leg, he returned home at the end of the war.

The prospect of not having a job and little money to begin a new life was the new reality. Yet, I believe, he had a new desire in his heart. I believe that he desired more than ever to find a wife, raise a family, and all that goes with it. His heart was full of the scars of the battlefield and he needed healing that could come from those around him. What better healing could come from finding someone who would love him and share emotions together?

Emotions play a huge role in the lives of people. Try to imagine how you may have felt after seeing lives lost in war. Imagine seeing your family for the first time after several years. Can you see tears of both joy and sorrow? Mom's home cooking must have been like a feast even without the meat. The war took a toll on my father that he would not willingly share when it came to harsh details. Nevertheless, Dad was now focused on moving on. For him that meant finding someone who could be his soul mate, bear his children, share his joy and be his encourager. Somehow, I think Dad just wanted to let go of the last four years and he buried much of that inside himself. Buried emotions usually don't stay buried forever, but for my father, he had learned in war to suck up the pain and forge on. My dad was my hero.

ABOUT MOM

Rae Wyland grew up an orphan. The family she knew did not include a mom or dad who loved her as she grew up. She would learn to be independent in many ways as she lived with other children in the orphanage. The dreams about what the future held may have been difficult to imagine, when her family was not there to encourage her. Yet, I know that she had them and am proud to say that she accomplished all that she set her eyes upon. The knowledge that my mother grew up in an orphanage was especially interesting. It is one thing to be raised by a single parent or relative. Being raised by a family member might provide a sense of security, but to think of living in a place where strangers provide your care seems so isolated.

Orphanages may provide wonderful care, yet the love of a mom and dad in daily doses seems to add so much more to all aspects of growing up, especially emotional. The thought of persevering without family providing those daily acts of encouragement made the story of my mother's childhood even more heartwarming. I can imagine each joyful event like graduation or college acceptance leaving a longing to share the event with those you love. How fortunate are those raised by a mom and dad. Rae must have had an inner strength and fortitude to move well beyond her conditions.

Rae was exceptionally intelligent. Mathematics and science were second nature to her. I learned from my father that she put herself through college and became an engineering manager at Bausch & Lomb in Rochester, New York. I found it interesting that Dad was not sure of her title, which I later learned from another family member. Dad knew she majored in the areas of math and science. He also knew that she made a lot more money than a farmer, who never went past the sixth grade. Dad was as proud for her as I think anyone could have been. It was an accomplishment that he would dwell on all through his life. How could two people of such diverse backgrounds meet and become soul mates?

I can only imagine the attraction had to do with her physical beauty and her desire to help others in need. I keep a picture of my mother on my dresser to view as a reminder of where I came from and just how pretty she was. Dad gave each of his sons the same picture with a three by five card hidden behind it. On the card he wrote about the fact that she came out of the orphanage and put herself through college. Dad would talk about her with a twinkle still in his eyes. She was everything that he desired and more. Those times in the trenches of war served to help them to really understand each other.

In 1945, the World's Fair was held in New York City. Dad wanted to take Rae there, but he doubted his car would make the trip without a breakdown. Not only did it need a lot of maintenance, but also the cost of repair went far beyond dad's limited budget. Despite the vehicle uncertainty, Dad called on her to make the journey from Rochester to New York City, a distance of nearly four hundred miles. The World's Fair was a big deal and seemingly worth the effort, despite a poor set of wheels. I picture my mom with enormous compassion as she insisted that they go, but in her vehicle. This must have thrilled him as he would have his date and not have to worry about the car breaking down. I can picture Mom enjoying every minute of the trip.

The trip turned out to be much more than just a date. Many hours of traveling in both directions allowed for a lot of conversation along the way. Dad would share with me later that this was the defining moment when he and mom made wedding plans. Dad was like a puppy dog, filled with love and playful energy as they shared that weekend together in New York. The phrase "I Love New York" could have been his cry then as well. He was now thirty-four and life finally offered a new direction.

There are things that I can only speculate on about Mom during those times. I have tried to empathize with her based on her background. She had a high IQ and I believe it also infected Dad. He was an avid bridge player, winning many awards. He would play with lesser players and get upset at their poor play, but not with my mom. She also learned the game and did very well for herself. Somehow, I think they complemented each other in intellectual things. Even though my dad did not get past the sixth grade, while my mom had a four-year college degree, they were intellectually compatible. Dad had an utmost respect for her in this area and I can see her encouraging him to better things as well.

In addition to her IQ she must have had a strong concern for the welfare of others and my dad was no exception.

Growing up in an orphanage may have instilled a caring attitude as each child drew strength from another. I believe it was this passion in my mom that truly had the most profound impact on my life and the lives of my two brothers. Mom had to have been the most incredible woman. She was dad's hero.

THEN THEY
WERE FIVE

The New York World Fair was history and they were married soon after. Life was wonderful again. Mom was the major breadwinner and her income was more than enough for them to succeed. She was only two years younger, but her biological clock was ticking loudly. In the span of the next five years they would lovingly mix sessions of bridge, warm romantic evenings, and the routine of work. They were devoted to each other and to fulfilling their dreams together. The honeymoon was hardly over and along came their first son, whom they named David.

David was a special child. He was more than just the first. He was the ultimate completion of the dream of having a family for both my mom and dad. They began nurturing this new life with all the love and compassion two parents could muster. I picture Mom after work, lovingly holding him and counting her blessings daily. I somehow can visualize her pouring out her wisdom as she read to him or tucked him in at night. Her days in the orphanage must have had a profound affect on her daily decisions to minister to his every need.

In the same way I see Dad taking care of him while she worked. I can picture Dave holding a fishing pole before his first birthday as he enjoyed going on fishing trips. Their early life together was spent in a small cottage on a fishing pond. I can see the joy in my dad's heart when Dave caught his first fish. Fishing was one thing that didn't require a great deal of money back then and an escape for my dad even before the war. Now he had the opportunity to share his fishing knowledge with his son and I can still see the beam in Dad's face.

Whenever Dad wanted to escape from the pressures of life it usually involved fishing. Each summer we looked forward to a week in the Thousand Islands area along the St. Lawrence River in upstate New York. I think it was more than just an escape, however. I think mom and dad wanted to get away to show off their family. I can see pride in their eyes. They would let Dave's hair grow without cutting it until the black and white photos made him appear more like a girl. I don't know if a girl was their first choice, but Dad says it was because Dave's hair was so curly and beautiful. I think the hair was a symbol, like a lion whose pride is its mane.

Then I came along about eighteen months later. I don't know why they chose the name Dennis for me, except that they both liked the name. Perhaps it was from the cartoon *Dennis the Menace* and forethought of things to come. Perhaps they liked the girl's name Denise and were disappointed that I was not a girl. It really doesn't matter as I can still sense a genuine love between all of us. I believe that

Mom showed an equal amount of love and affection for my brother and I. Now while Dad would be out fishing with Dave, Mom might be holding me singing lullabies.

I have pictures of my big brother with all his curls holding me on his lap. He seems to be saying, "I love my new brother… " as I am smiling with pride. I can picture the joy of my parents as they snap the picture. They seem to be saying, "It just doesn't get any better than this."

Then along came another boy. This time they named him Douglas. Our middle names bear significance to other family members in our heritage, but why another name starting with the letter D? We will be known as the three-Ds before three-dimensional viewing became a reality. I am thankful that he wasn't named Dilbert, however. Doug came about fourteen months after me. For a little over four months, after Doug celebrated his birthday, we were one year apart.

Growing up as three boys that close in age develops differences in our individuality. David was the firstborn and due to his role developed leadership tendencies. As second born, I seemed to let my older brother do his thing while I traveled a different road. My interests were closely similar to those of my dad. I think I was his shadow in many ways. Doug's motivation seemed to be just having fun. Yet, we were each endowed with solid math and science understanding from our mother.

My brother, David, has shared with me some of the events that he remembered about my mother. One of them involved a super eight video that showed our mother sitting playfully on the floor with three small boys climbing all over her. Mom's demeanor came across as joy. Perhaps it was after a long day of work and this was mom's way of unwinding. David described the video as one of delight for his brothers, himself, and our mother.

Now we are a family of five requiring a bigger cabin to live in, more fishing poles, and a lot more diapers. Dad was not the stereotype father who went to work, while his wife cared for the children. The roles were reversed and Dad accepted the challenge with joy. I picture my dad cooking the fresh perch caught that day from the pond in the backyard when my mom came home from work. I can see Mom reaching out to each of her sons after Dad tells her to relax before dinner is ready. Technical issues from Mom's work were probably replaced quite quickly with issues like the first words, first steps, or fishing exploits of her three boys. The American dream had begun.

WHY DID YOU HAVE TO GO, MOM?

The years until my younger brother's birth were filled with enormous joy, especially for our mom and dad. Raising three boys was also an awesome responsibility. Dad would later share with me how during the time when she was carrying Doug, she was searching for spiritual answers. I can speculate that she desired more for us than she could give physically. She had a tremendous knowledge of science and yet was still left with more unanswered questions.

Mom came from Jewish heritage. It seemed strange to me that Dad would fight in WWII to end the slaughtering of the Jews and then fall in love with one of their members. Equally odd is the fact that she had this background and now was searching for a higher meaning in her spiritual life. According to Biblical scriptures, they were God's chosen people and yet there was something missing in her spiritual journey. I feel so privileged to have her bloodline even today. Dad was brought up with a Christian mother, but was not a regular church attender. He allowed Mom to visit various denominations, but did not actively take part himself. I believe that mothers have something inside that desires only the very best for their children. I believe that my mom knew that there was one area that she felt inadequate to fulfill, that was our spiritual needs, and sought help. Her Jewish teaching seemed incomplete. At any rate while carrying her third child she did some earnest soul searching, which would also impact her entire family later in life.

The result of Rae's searching was a new faith. She accepted Jesus Christ as her Savior and Lord in a Baptist church in Rochester, New York. This was a defining moment for both Mom and Dad. The year was 1948.

Then came three horrible words: "You have cancer." If those words were spoken today, we might be more hopeful, but not in 1950. Suddenly the whole world was turned upside down. The dreams for tomorrow were shattered, but even worse was the fact that she was the wage earner. Whatever it took to save her life would be taken from their savings and then after she was gone, there would be nothing to replenish it.

I never knew my mom as she passed shortly after I turned three. Dave remembers her for a short time. David told me that he remembers the day Mom died. Three boys stood by her bedside. Mom looked at each of us and muttered, "I… I… " It was only one word, but David said that it was as if she wanted to say, "I love you" to each of her sons. Sometimes I wish that I could have known her even for that brief period to formulate something to remember her by. About fifty years later I would have a counselor tell me what I must have felt at the time of her death. The sudden loss of affection, her gentle voice, and all those things that emulated love towards me were suddenly gone. A scared little boy was screaming, "Come back." Mom's death would shape my emotional life forever. I am not sure how much caressing was done from my father, but I am reasonably sure that Mom did so tirelessly. Suddenly it was taken away and three boys desired it back.

Dad lost even more. His soul mate was gone. His dreams were shattered. He was broke without a job and he had three boys to care for. I can only imagine that Dad must have felt as if life had ended. His first desire was to get help from family members while he secured work. By this time his brothers and sisters were busy raising families of their own and could not provide the support he needed. His mother was also busy handling many duties alone. Dad was able to secure work as a machinist in a small machine shop along with finding a one-room apartment nearby. By this time he had filed for bankruptcy and was without a vehicle.

The rejection from his family left Dad bitter. This bitterness would hold him hostage for much of his later life. Dealing with rumbling emotions is easier when family is there in times of need. Imagine the emotional unrest when the support is not to be found. We are responsible for our own feelings and choices. Dad had learned through the war that when a comrade was in need and you were there, then you helped meet the need. Perhaps that training affected his decision to be bitter. Whatever the reasoning, Dad chose to be resentful to those who supported him in the bunkers at Normandy through their letters. Dad would carry the same ill feelings toward a bridge partner, who fails to show up for

Legacy of Love 29

a game. The loss of his soul mate affected far more than his dreams. It almost cost him his very soul.

As for three boys we were placed in a foster home about twenty miles away. Dad insisted that we were not to be separated and finding a single place for all of us at reasonable cost was difficult. The first place where I remember the name of the person there was not the first home. Her name was Faye and our memories are anything but loving. When Dad would get information that we were not being treated well, he would seek new locations for us to stay. It took years before we found something that provided nurturing.

Some of the memories shared between my brothers and I include two significant events. First, we can recall living at Faye's and having unbreakable plates broken over our heads. We can remember the nightmares, the crying, and the physical pain. We remember pleading with Dad to take us with him each time he came to visit. I think that our screaming only increased the fury unleashed by Faye on us.

The second more vivid event involves several occasions where we were placed in a room with the belief that there was a taped up mummy on a shelf that was going to get us. For me that place was like a pantry. For Doug it was like a garage. At any rate the psycho movies of today are G-rated in comparison as far as we were concerned. I can remember beating on the base of a seemingly ten-feet-high door and screaming until I became hoarse and without strength. I remember believing that this mummy was going to leap off the shelf at any moment and swallow me up. I was deathly afraid.

These events caused deep emotional scars that I carried long into my married life. It would be my hope and prayer that others, who are going through similar events, can recognize that they need help and find it. Dr. Phil McGraw speaks about "defining moments" in our lives which shape who we are. This is one along with the loss of my mother. Only recently did I learn that emotionally I was screaming *Doesn't anybody love me?* and *Doesn't anyone care about me?*

Why did you have to go, Mom?

A FAMILY AGAIN

Foster homes did keep three brothers together and for that we are grateful. I often wonder what would have happened to us if we were separated and did not have each other to lean on. We had our trials but we also had times when we were able to enjoy just being together. The most memorable times, while apart from Dad, occurred on a farm. The Harris family took the reins as our last foster parents and life began to improve. We were now with a family who shared Christian values and allowed us to be kids. We shared responsibilities around the farm and began to enjoy activities together like jumping off a barn loft onto a high pile of hay. I don't think that we were as adamant about leaving there when Dad would visit.

We learned how to milk a cow as well as ride it. Taking warm milk directly from a cow was a common sight. One Guernsey cow had been given the name Old Betsy. My brothers and I would take turns riding Old Betsy down a lane toward an apple orchard. On more than one occasion, while I was aboard, Dave would twist Old Betsy's tail turning a mild milk cow into a charging steed. Holding on was a challenge. The ride would typically end in the orchard, where the apple tree limbs would be too low to duck. I don't recall ever being hurt, but I remember three boys laughing so hard that our sides ached.

Now the visits would come with a new addition. Dad had not been able to visit as often as he had wanted because of transportation issues. Lena was barely five feet tall and wore high heels so she could reach the gas pedal on her new Chevrolet. She had been seeing Dad and helping him to get on his feet after the bankruptcy. Her car was a welcome sight at the farm, especially one day when it carried a new Schwinn red bicycle. One by one three boys would start pedaling and falling into the nearest straw pile. It didn't take too long until we were able to ride without help.

It was also not too long after that when they came to take us to live with them. She became the only mother I ever knew as she agreed to be Dad's wife and our mom. What a joy for each of us. We were finally a family again. We still enjoyed visiting the Harris farm when we could. That was the only foster home that we felt that way about. It was a new beginning and my brothers and I looked forward to it. David was in the fifth grade. I was in fourth and Doug in third. It seemed like we had just met Lena and she was our mom.

David was especially close to the Harris family, who took in many foster care children. Each one was treated as one of their own. When Mrs. Harris died, Dave was deeply moved and pedaled the Schwinn bike about twenty miles to pay his respects. David had memories of our mother,

Rae, and the passing of Mrs. Harris may have been like losing another mother.

Together they were able to purchase a home so we did not have to share a one-room apartment. Dave and I were in one bedroom, while Doug had his own. I remember helping my dad paint some of the rooms, which were deep red in color. It took many coats to get the red out. I think it was also the reason they were able to get the house at such a low price. With Dad's credit I don't believe they would qualify for much more, but to us it was a beautiful sight. I also think that I got more paint on me than on the wall. It was the start of my character building, as I would find myself looking for opportunities to be with Dad. I longed for those things that I missed even though I was not sure what they were. Somehow I knew that being around Dad offered the most satisfaction. We stayed in that home until I started high school (ninth grade). At that time we moved to a larger home with more outside space to run. The house was also near several farms, which would further serve to shape my future.

Dad was a Rochester Horseshoe Champion and I would watch him toss ringers in the yard. He paced off forty feet and set the stakes near some sickle pear trees. He would then place a pear at the base of one stake and throw a ringer without touching the pear. I learned to throw a pretty competitive horseshoe at the local picnic spot, but it was pale compared to his. He would spot me fifteen points to a game of twenty-one and I can count one hand the number of times that I beat him. I remember one day when I threw five consecutive ringers and he got three points by throwing six. Yet I enjoyed every moment of it.

We still had our vacations on the water along the St. Lawrence. Dave, Doug, and I would take flashlights to the nearest golf course to hunt for nightcrawlers. This was usually a gold mine due to the watering systems employed by the course. We would get a penny each and it would not be uncommon to gather several hundred worms. We would pack them in soaked newspapers and ice for the vacation trip. We loved to fish and I think Dad loved to share the experience with us.

Our new mom was not openly affectionate towards us, but we welcomed her and called her *mom*. She did not replace the things that I felt taken away as a three-year-old as I would learn later. My emotional aches needed to be reassured through affection and I would go on searching for those answers as I pursued my marital dreams. Nevertheless, I would like to share a fish story involving my new mom. My brothers and I were at the vacation spot fishing off a small dock. As I attempted to cast I found myself going into the water with the rod. Mom saw me and ran to the dock. I had a very short brush cut and remember not being afraid, watching fish swimming under the water. The next thing I knew I was being pulled out of the water by my hair. The event was amazing since my hair was barely long enough to grab. Somehow she was able to get me out of the water.

Our new family was doing well as was evident by the report cards from three boys. We were all well above average with mostly As and Bs, but Dave only desired the A. He made the National Honor Society and won a full scholarship to a local college. I was happy with As and Bs as long as I could go work on the nearby farms after school and weekends. I was the ambitious one and did not want to be a burden on my family for the things I wanted, like my first car. I would take many math classes in my junior and senior year so that I wouldn't have to do homework, as it seemed to come so natural for me. I had a lawn mowing, snow shoveling, and leaf-raking route along with various farm jobs.

On Friday evenings, Mom and Dad would go out leaving us a dollar to spend at the store for goodies. It was about a two and a half mile bike ride and we would take turns as to who would go. Usually, I would donate another dollar from my earnings in trade for not having to make the ride. We would pig out on popsicles, popcorn, candy bars, and all those other things that we shouldn't have. It was something we looked forward to as well as did Mom and Dad. Often they would go have a fish fry together and then go their separate ways. Dad would play bridge while Mom would play Bingo. Then they would meet and come home. I don't remember whether the house was left in the same condition as when they left, but we were full. I always felt good about the fact that they were able to regularly do the things they enjoyed without us and thought it was something that I would like when I had a family.

I remember one incident at school when my brothers and I were all called into the principal's office with Mom. I expected the worst, as I am sure my brothers did as well. Being called into the principles office was usually deemed as a negative event. The principal began with words like, "I want you to look at these three report cards." They were new and we had not seen them. Even though we didn't think that we had any bad grades, the negative thoughts still crept through our minds. The principal then said something like "You should be very proud of them. What a wonderful job they are doing." Mom would share that story over and over for many years to come. It was a source of pride for her and we breathed a sigh of relief.

We had our ups and downs but we were a family. That meant everything to Dad and us.

THREE DIFFERENT BROTHERS

We would graduate on three consecutive years and each take different routes for our futures. Dave took full advantage of his scholarship and put himself through college. He also joined the U.S. Navy and completed his service after graduating. He graduated near the top of his class. One source of emotional pain for him was in how Dad expressed his approval. Dave expected more than Dad would give to each of us for the extra effort that it took to reach these higher goals. Dad didn't recognize Dave any differently than he did the rest of us. Remember he never went past the sixth grade. Therefore, graduating was an enormous accomplishment, let alone with high marks. He was very proud of Dave, but didn't know how to express it.

The desire for affirmation is one effect that I believe came from the loss of a parent, especially a mother, early in a child's maturing years. We had affirmation and then suddenly it was taken from us. Children make internal decisions about what they like based on experience. If they like something, they want it and will go to all lengths to attain it. As an adult, we may still be crying or throwing a tantrum, but with different expressions. The need to be recognized for who we are, what we stand for, our accomplishments, and other areas, is normal. Having that need drive us emotionally can have huge consequences, as we become adults. I believe three boys had that inner desire heightened after losing a mother and then experiencing rejection from those taking her place.

Sometimes the applause of others is a good thing. There are other times when it can be a detriment, as we have to have it to be happy. Each of us desires some form of affirmation from others, but we can also take pride in knowing that we accomplished our objective, whether others recognized it or not. Remember in chapter two when our real mother put herself through college. I don't know if there were many at her graduation that understood the magnitude of that, but she did. I like the verse in Matthew 6:19–21 that says:

> Do not store up for yourselves treasures on earth, where moth and rust destroy, and where thieves break in and steal. But store up for yourselves treasures in heaven where moth and rust do not destroy and where thieves do not break in and steal. For where your treasure is, there your heart will be also.

This speaks to our hearts as being the source of our treasures. When we place that responsibility on others we jeopardize losing the very things that we cherish. God knows our hearts even when others don't and He won't let us down. Likewise, I believe that when we receive our reward from others we tend to withhold our treasures from heaven. The overwhelming desire for affirmation can be a real source of pain, when not received. I have learned to trust myself and accept purposeful tasks as challenges. It is far less threatening to me to perform a task and then look at the accomplishment with just the satisfaction that I did it. If I waited until someone else affirmed that it was good, then my level of satisfaction would be greatly reduced until the affirmation was received.

THOUGHT:

The first chapter of the Bible talks about creation. After each day, God said "... and it was good." After the sixth day He said, "It was very good." He didn't have others to give Him the credit that, perhaps He desired. He was his own critic. I am thankful that He didn't look at even one day of creation and say that it was not good. He took pride in the design and gave himself credit for success.

We can be our own positive reinforcement or our worst critic. Somehow, we need to learn that anything worth doing is worth doing without the approval process of others. A mother changes a baby's diaper because it is far better than the alternative. She doesn't ask whether she needs approval first. The need for affirmation is both normal and desired. I believe that it can also be excessive when carried too far. It places an enormous responsibility on those around us. It would be presumptuous on our part to believe that others understand our need for positive feedback. The child inside us may be screaming for something, while our expectation is that we are understood. When we don't get the reinforcement that we desire, we often regress and our emotional well being suffers the consequences. We may not have understood this concept as a child, but I believe my brothers and I grew up with an oversensitive need for affirmation. I further believe that our actions solicited a response, whether we knew it at the time or not. The effect on the people around us may well have been one of isolation and rejection, traits that would pour more coals on our emotional being.

David graduated from high school with a National Honor Society scholarship. He used it to attend the Brockport State University in New York near where we lived. In addition, he enlisted in the Navy's ROTC program, which paralleled the four years of college and an additional two-year tour upon graduation. The navy would station David at the Key West base in Florida. Dave's love of fishing and the ocean was not diminished, but rather enhanced in Key West. Upon discharge he took a teaching position on Key Largo, specializing in math and science. Dave's career path would keep him in southern Florida, where he would raise three children of his own along with his wife, Jan.

When I graduated from high school, I did not know what I wanted to do in life. I wanted to test the waters of the work world and see what happens. I had my car, my license, my diploma, and a well-diversified work experience. They knew me where Dad worked and hired me to handle a host of apartment repairs like plumbing, electrical, painting, and drywall work. I had done many of these things by helping Dad at home. After a few months I was offered a better paying job at Eastman Kodak Company, where I ultimately retired from after thirty-two years (four of which was military). After only there ten months I decided to join the Air Force. The Vietnam War was in progress and I thought that if I had to serve, then I should be able to decide a path. The Air Force offered electronic training and that interested me. I spent thirty-six weeks learning autopilot and heading systems for B-52 and KC135 refueling tankers. Then I spent most of my time learning the trade in Michigan and Goose Bay, Labrador, near Newfoundland, Canada.

The Air Force taught me a lot about electronics. It also taught me to respect authority, being part of a team, and how to take charge. I really enjoyed the challenge of the job, the teamwork, and the camaraderie of fellow airmen. We were like family. I was also enjoying the time away from my family in New York. Sometimes we stay so close to family that we fail to see the whole picture. When I would come home on leave, Mom and Dad would treat me in a whole new way. I was no longer a little child. It felt good. I was also happy to leave again as the welcome wore off. Dad understood military service and I could sense his pride in me as I served my country.

Then there was Doug, who decided to go to college to avoid the draft. He was eager to get away from Mom and Dad and the restrictions placed by them on him. He didn't know what he wanted to do in life but decided to spend four years searching. New York City offered the benefits of attending a state school, while still four hundred miles from home. So off he went. I don't know everything that went on there, but I would see him return from time to time with distinct changes. Mom would call him a hippy with his long hair. Ironically, each of us would welcome long hair today as we have developed baldness on top. I saw him as the partygoer. He seemed to spend his available time on the social scene.

Four years later the Army drafted him. That was only fitting since his other brothers were in different branches of the armed forces. He would not complete his degree until long after completing his tour of duty. He was also the only one of us sent to Vietnam. Each of us went different routes to find our vocation in life. Dave became a math and science teacher on the Florida Keys. Doug went to work as a machine programmer in Rochester. Rochester remains Doug's home, where he raised two children with his wife, Anne.

I returned to Eastman Kodak where I went through the electrical apprenticeship, became an electrician, a technician, and finally an engineer. I spent twelve years attending night school at a technical college in Rochester for an electrical-mechanical degree. Three brothers became men with families and grandchildren. I am sure our mom in heaven would be smiling over our accomplishments.

A NEW DREAM BEGINS

At some point in our lives we begin to seek our dreams of having our own families. It was Christmas time 1967 when I decided to spend it with Mom and Dad. I was feeling pretty down on any new relationships after being dumped by a girl from Illinois on Thanksgiving of that year. I invited an airman, who would have been stuck on the base over the holiday, to come home with me. Our home always welcomed our friends, which is a tradition that I have maintained over the years. The trip covered five hundred miles from Michigan to Rochester, New York, through Ontario, Canada. In good weather the drive would be scenic and enjoyable. Winter had only just begun so the snow squalls, cold winds, and icy roads would hinder return trips in the months to follow. I didn't know that the return trip would instill a desire to bear the elements in the wintry weeks ahead.

One of the towns that the trip from Michigan to New York would include was London, Ontario. I would refer to London as the Snow Belt of Canada. The trip would enter London from the north, often with little or no snow on the ground. Within a few short miles the snow seemed to mount and the visibility neared zero. It was not unusual to leave the town with two feet of snow on the ground. The ten-mile stretch would take an hour or more, but once through London the snow would disappear. Whenever I would drive through in thirty minutes or less, I would breathe a sigh of relief. January through April of 1968 would provide ample opportunities for sighs.

A fellow airman and I would arrive on December 23, 1967. Dave was at home on leave as well. We discussed doing something together and Dave suggested bowling. He was dating a girl and wanted to know if I would like a date as well. His girlfriend, Jan, had a roommate who may be coaxed to join us. I said that she could be a date for my friend but that I was not anxious to date for a while. Little did I know the events of that night would change my life forever. We went bowling, but I did not see my friend making any advances in the directions of his date. I thought she was beautiful. Her name was Dottie. The evening ended with my brother and I staying at the girl's apartment until late, while my airman friend was dropped off at our dad's house. I learned later that he was in the progress of proposing to a girl from his hometown and was simply content to bowl and watch TV. That was just fine with me.

Dottie was more than beautiful. She seemed to touch all the right emotional buttons in me. I felt alive and recharged. We discussed our previous relationships and learned that we had a lot in common in that area. Her old boyfriend had recently dumped her as well. As I look back on those days I can see that we both may have had our emotional blindfolds on. Was it love at first sight or just the effect of relational rebounds? All I knew is that I really wanted to know her completely.

Dottie and Jan came from small towns outside the Rochester area. They were neighbors at the age of eight. Jan would move to a nearby town, but they would remain high school classmates. When they graduated they desired to remain friends and decided to share an apartment together in the big city. Soon after they graduated they did just that. Jan pursued a nursing career, while Dottie applied her typing skills and took a job at a loan office. Jan and Dottie enjoyed a long-term friendship that has grown closer over the years. Leaving home soon after high school without going to college may be somewhat unusual today, but the sixties seemed to be more adventurous. There was a new world out there to discover, that living in a rural town may not offer. Dottie was out to discover it.

Our meeting that Christmas was a source of conversation for the girls to share together during the months that followed. The idea of marrying brothers and being best friends forever was also discussed. I would wish that everyone could find such a friendship.

The months that followed were filled with a long distance romance. Dottie and I shared a great deal about our lives through long letters and expensive phone bills. If wireless phones were available back then we would have saved money with the unlimited calling plan. At least once a month I would have the duty of "Charge of Quarters" at the living quarters where we stayed on the base. It was a twelve-hour shift from six in the evening, where we were responsible for staying alert protecting the barracks. When things were pretty quiet I would begin a long letter and finish it at the end of the shift. I located a roll of four foot wide brown wrapping paper and I would begin to write using normal letter script. The letters would unroll to nine or ten feet at times. My thoughts, details of the barracks, what was on TV, and anything else that came to mind filled the letter. It made the twelve hours pass quickly.

On one occasion I cut a three feet circle out of the brown paper and decided to write a letter by continuously turning the paper as I wrote starting at the outside. Although it was not ten feet long it took longer to read it, as Dottie would get caught in its web. She first went home over lunch to get her mail in anticipation of a letter and then tried to read it through the interruptions of work. Eventually she would find herself stretched out on her apartment floor turning the letter. We laughed together over the phone as we discussed it.

On another occasion, Dottie sent to me a typed letter on toilet paper. I thought it was amazing that the typewriter keys did not cause the paper to tear. The letter was a lot easier to read than the circle, but just as enjoyable. Our courtship was a long distance one to be sure. Her letters would often end with words like, "I am going to jump into my mini jet and fly up to see you." Today that could be a reality, but in 1968 it was certainly a dream. I sensed that her heart desired to be with me as mine longed to be with her.

I also learned that Dottie was an excellent cook. Before I would leave on Sunday she would usually make a big meal. I rarely would begin my drive hungry and she would make baked goods for me to take along as well. Usually after a big meal we tend to get sleepy and that would not be good for the drive back. I think I was on such a high from just being with her that the emotional high kept me awake for most of the trip. The last hour or so may have been the toughest. I would finally crash from exhaustion on Monday night after work, but my thoughts of the trip throughout that day would sustain me even without much sleep. Those trips were so important to me as I needed to hold her and for her to hold me, something that letters would not do. I still desire that oneness.

In the spring of '68 Dottie and Jan decided to make the drive to see me. Earlier, I had told her that if she ever came to see me, I would have a surprise for her. I think she liked surprises. When she returned on that occasion, she had picked out her engagement ring and we began planning the next step—our wedding. I still had two years remaining in the service so this meant some sacrifices for her to make as well. She would have to pick up and move to Michigan and leave family and friends if the date set was before I got out. We agreed on an August date only months away, so the decision to move was done. Our parents were not very well off so in addition some financial arrangements would need to be made. Dottie was a member of a small Free Methodist church in the Rochester area so the choice of church and pastor would be an easy one. My brothers and Jan would have to be included in the wedding. I would be the first of three brothers to tie the knot.

The decisions were made. The plans were set and we were married August 17, 1968. It was a significant date as we had originally planned the day to be August 24. Pastor Lester Gales informed us that he had a vacation with his family scheduled on the twenty-fourth and wondered if we would consider the seventeenth. We agreed, as we didn't want him to leave his family during their vacation. We returned from our honeymoon in the Pennsylvania Pocono resort on the twenty-fourth and awoke to some earth-shaking news. Pastor Gales had drowned on the twenty-fourth trying to save his son after the canoe they were in capsized. The event would be with me for the rest of my life. No matter what we were going through in our married life, I could always fall back to that day. I could not shake the feeling that Pastor Gale's death was not without purpose. He died on the very day that we originally planned for our wedding. It was as if destiny made a claim on our lives together.

I was just a young man twenty years of age, but already mature beyond my years. Dad had to sign for me to tie the knot, as the legal age for men in New York was twenty-one. We could be soldiers for our country at the age of eighteen, but we were not responsible enough to make a decision on our own regarding marriage. I believe that I had a greater appreciation for people and commitments than others my age due to my childhood experiences. Two years in the military had a strong influence on my level of maturity. I was more than ready to accept the responsibilities of being a husband and provider. Letter writing and phone conversations could now be replaced by a closeness that I could only imagine. I had never shared my body with a woman. The story of the birds and the bees was not shared in any detail and I was a bit apprehensive. The idea of being near the one I had fallen in love with was all I needed to face whatever would happen next.

THE DREAM BECOMES REALITY

The long distance romance was now over. We were a couple living off the base in a one-bedroom cottage. The weather was similar to Rochester, but new friends would need to be made to call it home. Unfortunately, I had been issued orders to spend six weeks in Goose Bay, Labrador, shortly after returning from our honeymoon. We had reserved a cottage and hardly had enough time to get settled when I had to leave. There she was in a strange place with few acquaintances. Dottie could have considered going back to New York, but elected to tough it out and find a job to occupy her time. She found one at a local financial office and was able to start work quickly. Working helped her to pass the time and gave her an extra sense of self-worth, as she would add income to a somewhat meager airman's income.

The time apart would go quickly for me as I put in long hours on the flight line and continued writing letters to my new bride. Dottie's letters were sustaining, but I sensed that when I returned we would have our first decision to face together. She had seen a mouse (maybe more) and wanted to move from that cottage. A man might set the traps, catch the critter, and end the problem. I don't think that would work for most women. If there is one there are many. Mice are dirty and carry diseases. When I returned we found another place that became our home until I was discharged. It was one of several small green log cabins outside the base with Air Force couples occupying the others as well. We made friends there and enjoyed our new home.

The honeymoon was over and we began to discover more about each other than can be expressed in letters. Many things were not easy for Dottie to express and I was impetuous when I thought there was something that needed to be shared. Slowly I began feeling shut out from her. It was both frightening and frustrating. When I would ask for clarity or more information over something that was said, she would retreat. I longed for something called intimacy with my wife and began to feel rejection and isolation. Physical pleasure was not the issue. Rather, there was something inside that was causing me to feel a pain that I did not feel before and it hurt. The more I would seek answers, the more rejected I would feel. Understanding what was happening was a process that would unfold over the next thirty years.

One of the purposes of this writing is to help others understand what it took thirty years for me to understand. Understanding our emotions begins with who we are based on where we've been. For me my first significant event was the loss of my real mother. We are often well versed in the physical reality of things as we can see, touch, or feel in those areas. Our emotional side is quite different and can be far more explosive. We can't apply normal senses to our emotions and until we understand what is really happening, we can easily be trapped by those feelings.

Mom was taken from me at age three. I speak for anyone who loses a parent or close relative at an early age. The feelings of safety and security when Mom held me were gone. The words of encouragement were also gone. Then came the years of abuse from foster homes including a mummy that created an enormous fear. Being shut out from those we love is difficult to bear. Being shut in with demons is even worse. I can now picture the little boy in me still screaming, "Doesn't anybody out there love me?" or "Doesn't anyone care about me?"

I didn't realize it at the start of my marriage, but I now understand that I was screaming those things then when I felt rejection with my wife. I longed for intimacy and somehow that desire was not hers as well. Dottie may have wanted it, but not in the same time frame as I did. When I became frustrated my voice would elevate and she would be the one feeling pressured. This was not something that I intended by moving forward, but my actions caused my wife to move away, the very thing that I was trying to fix. For anyone who may have felt rejection, perhaps our story is for you.

I think now that I desired to have a special oneness with my new bride that mirrored the one felt with my mother during the first three years of my life. I saw the future filled with hope, joy, and love with moments of sadness being shared to lighten the load. I could picture us sharing our dreams, consoling each other during trials, and shedding tears of joy during the triumphs. I longed for a closeness that would not keep secrets and an openness to share our feelings without fear. I desired no competition, only complementation. She completed in me all the things that I felt that I missed from childhood and I wanted to do the same for her. When Dottie would pull away, I felt incomplete and isolated. It would leave me feeling totally helpless. Inside I was crying out, "Don't you love me?" and "Don't you care about me? Can't you understand how deeply I am hurt?" The answers to my questions would not come and I would push the hurts deep inside. I learned how to suck it up and focus on the next day. I couldn't let my emotions affect my parenthood and my role as a husband and provider. Tomorrow was always another day and I would tell myself to not let past feelings ruin it.

Most mornings, when I would awake and see her beside me, I would get a feeling of thankfulness to know she was my wife and companion. When I would return from a day at work, I would anticipate the warm embrace with excitement. I can picture Dad having the same feelings and thoughts when Mom would arrive home after her day from work. My career path would place me in a similar pattern as Mom. I would apply technical thoughts to my work in the electronics arena, which is far removed from what I would need as a husband at home. The change for me was quite different and the welcomed hug would serve to separate work from my role at home.

Many relationships in the modern world are even more stressful and distinct with respect to separation of vocation and marital responsibilities. Too often we carry the concerns of the workplace into our homes without the means to break the chain. I believe that marriages are stretched to the breaking point by money and its pursuit more than any other thing. I believe that when people fail to recognize their spouse's needs things collapse. When needs are not being met, human nature will seek to find alternatives. Affairs, one-night-stands, casual cups of coffee with the opposite sex, and other options will surface.

I was committed to my wife and my obligations. Like Dad, I desired to be a man of my word. My wedding vows were sacred and not to be broken. Therefore, when I felt a separation forming between my wife and I, I would consider only those choices that would help mend the situation. Extra-marital affairs did not meet those criteria. I believed that I needed to communicate in any way I could, what I was going through with the one whom I felt separated. My impatience along with my desire to *fix it* would also be my emotional dilemma. The harder I would try, the more I would feel separated. There were times when I would even try isolation by just not talking in hopes that she would come forward and share from her heart. Rarely did those times work. When I felt separated from Dottie, I would refer to it as a *wall* between us. It was so hard to describe, but somehow the child inside me continued to scream, "Don't you love me?" and "Don't you care about me?" For me it was as automatic as ducking when the head senses danger approaching, except it was coming from my heart. I never stopped loving my wife or dreaming the dream that we would become an *us* emotionally.

THEN THERE WERE FOUR

By the time I returned from Labrador, Dottie was well settled in her job. She was happy that she was able to supplement our income in that manner and excited about turning our residence into a home. An airman E-4s income was somewhat limited then and her salary would help provide items considered luxuries otherwise. We agreed to postpone having children for a time so that we could get to know each other better.

We decided to keep her car as it was in better condition and newer than the one I had. So I sold mine. Her '64 Ford Falcon convertible was pretty sharp until the winter salt began its decay. The old Ford was becoming less reliable and I learned that a reliable vehicle was high on my wife's needs. With her income and a part-time bartending job off the base on weekends, we were able to purchase a new '69 Olds Cutlass. It had a Hurst three-speed on the floor, bucket seats, and a 350 engine that would rumble with excitement. Its light green metallic finish seemed to glisten no matter how dirty it got. It was a major purchase that we made together and one that we both loved. Living in Michigan offered some pricing advantages in buying a GM car. The thirty-six payments were a whopping ninety dollars and we were able to double them up due to our added income.

My role as provider was now a reality and I intended to excel in that area. I think that I found an area that I could be successful as a husband and also stimulate Dottie into a higher level of communication. It was as though her love language was in the area of gifts and I loved to speak it. Perhaps I felt that if I could speak her language, then she would make the effort to speak mine. I was committed to keep the lines of communication open.

In the spring of '69 I received orders to go to Thailand. My last year in the service appeared to keep us separated and we discussed new plans for the future. Dottie decided to quit her job and prepared to move back to Rochester. I agreed, as I wanted her to at least be near her family while I was on the other side of the world. I enjoyed my work as an autopilot technician, so I wasn't that disturbed by the opportunity to continue somewhere else, even Southeast Asia. I was more concerned about my wife and her needs. Besides, the lost art of letter writing would be rekindled. My country needed me. My wife needed me. My need to be needed as a child was now in duplicate.

The day drew near for me to leave and suddenly my orders were cancelled. I now had new orders to go to Labrador again for just two weeks. I didn't understand why. Perhaps my friends in Labrador requested me personally.

Perhaps I had a guardian angel watching over me and knew the trip to Thailand would have long-term future consequences that I would not see. Whatever the reason, we had to make new choices.

No longer would Dottie have to go to Rochester with all our belongings. She could consider a two-week vacation there in my absence instead, since she no longer had a job. We could still maintain our car payments on my salary, but I don't remember whether we continued paying two months at a time.

One significant result of this situation was the decision to begin a family. Birth control was stopped and very quickly we learned that we were to be parents before my career would be over in the Air Force. The medical benefits in the military were better than any HMO plan. My only regret today was that I could not watch the birthing process. I think that policy has since been changed. Moms were kept with child in the hospital for four to five days and all I had to pay for was Dottie's food. I remember that I got change back from a ten-dollar bill.

Dottie did not appear to be nine months along when the baby was due. The child was small and her weight gain was less than twenty pounds for the entire time. We began focusing on those things for the child like nursery items, clothes, and what diapers to use. We decided to use cloth diapers and then disposable ones when we were away. This decision was interesting, as our son would cling to his buddy, which was any cloth diaper. We had an abundant supply of buddies. The day grew near and the contractions started five minutes apart. It was her exact due date.

Off to the base hospital we went. I think those last few days were filled with such anticipation that I probably slept with my clothes on and the car packed. I was not going to be late for this one. We arrived around seven in the morning and I remember the attending nurse saying that Dottie was not ready to have this child due to her small size. A few moments later the nurse came back after an examination with the words, "She has dilated four centimeters so we have to keep her." The excitement of the moment was wonderful. I could hardly control myself. My wife told me to go get something to eat since she would be a while in the exam room.

I left for the commissary to have breakfast and pick up the newspaper. I tried to prepare for what I perceived to be a long wait. This was our first child and we were told that they take the longest. Besides, Dottie was only about 120 pounds with child. I think I had the vision that small people took longer to deliver. At any rate I was prepared for the wait. I returned within an hour and Dottie was now in the waiting room where I could be with her. I remember opening my newspaper to begin passing the time, while looking for ways to help her with the contractions. Little did I know that the newspaper would be an instrument in that process? Dottie's stomach began reacting to this new birth in a way that I did not expect and the paper was there to catch the result. Nevertheless, I would no longer be passing the time as I had planned.

At 11:07 in the morning, Jeffrey David was born. He was less than six pounds, eighteen and one half inches long and had big feet (at least that was the doctor's reply). He was healthy, Mom was doing well and I was euphoric. He was so beautiful and I was so proud. When I left that day, I hurried to buy cigars and candy to commemorate the occasion. It was March 9, 1970, and snow was still on the ground. I ran from log cabin to cabin where we lived, knocking on doors, and sharing our joy. Even falling flat on my butt from an icy sidewalk did not lessen my zeal. I was a father.

The birth of a child has to be one of nature's top wonders. We seem to immediately focus all our energies on this helpless little child and watch in awe at each new development. Mother's seem to have an even closer relationship as they had a nine-month head start in that area. Our life took on a new direction and we both looked forward to the future. Somehow at least for a time, I put aside the emotional issues between husband and wife and began to focus on my new role as Dad. Suddenly, the future opened even more doors of opportunities, like school, baseball tossing, ice cream cones, and diapers. I even shared the load when it came to changing the diapers, although it took a little time to understand how to make the proper folds. I think some people would know who changed our son last by how the diaper was secured.

In August we were now civilians. I enjoyed the service and contemplated re-enlisting, but the fear of being sent to a foreign country caused my wife to desire returning home. My old job was guaranteed, along with four years of cost-of-living wage increases. I knew that I wanted to pursue a career in electronics and my job, as a messenger, did not meet that goal. I also knew that the company had a highly rated apprentice program and was determined to apply for the electrical area. I began working the eleven in the evening shift when I returned, as it was the only opening. We secured an apartment with the same person who held the lease for Dottie and Jan before the wedding. Life on the outside was now a reality.

To supplement my income I would take on additional work. Dottie decided to apply her typing skills again, this time at a local hospital in the admitting department. She would work weekends, while I watched the baby. For Dottie, those times were special as I was assured of having two days (actually nights, as Dottie worked the night shift) of bonding with our son. That was very important to my wife. I think her mom did most of the child rearing and she felt Dad should be involved regularly in that area. I didn't mind the responsibility, but there were times when I worked long hours during the week and didn't feel like I was able to rest. I would call her at the hospital with every new moment of joy or other event discovered as a dad. I think Dottie looked forward to those calls, as her voice seemed to perk up with each shared experience.

When she would return, I would be half asleep. As soon as the garage door would open, my body would somehow shut down as if to say, "Mom's home so I can go to sleep." Prior to that I think I would have heard a pin drop. Dottie would carry on a conversation with me when she came into our bedroom after work. I would answer her questions until my answers became silly and incoherent. Then she would laugh. I think she was still laughing in the morning and it caused her to share the story with me. I remember laughing as well and it felt good. I would not remember anything about the conversation.

Our landlord was not taking care of the problem areas, causing me to consider looking for a house. We had only a few hundred dollars in our savings account and I was determined to find ways to earn the money needed for closing and the down payment to secure a house. We started looking and seeking answers from a Realtor and I pursued our dream. On Friday nights I would earn twenty to twenty-five dollars cutting up horseradish at one of my old farm job locations. I pumped gas on weekends before Dottie went to work and swept floors at a local car dealership from eight till noon after working all night during the week. I don't remember when I caught up on sleep, but I was determined to do whatever it takes. We were able to buy a two-bedroom house near where I worked and closed within only a few months. Our savings when it was all over was even higher than when we started.

Soon after getting the house I gave up the extra jobs. New owners took over the horseradish business and decided to end my services. During the same time the apprentice program called to let me know that I would be in the next electrical program. In addition, my military service provided training supplement dollars and the apprenticeship was considered training. Dottie continued working and I was pursuing my career dreams working daytime hours instead of nights. Somehow, we understood our duties as parents, and did them well. I was providing for those I loved, my career was focused, and we had our first house.

I was in my final year as an apprentice. Graduation meant a large salary increase and the title of electrician. My military benefits would end, but the income would still be higher. Then we got the news that we would be parents a second time. We had discussed having two children as a goal and having a son and a daughter would be absolutely wonderful. Neither Dottie nor I had any sisters, so I think we were resigned to the fact that this child would again be a boy. We even read articles on how to have a girl and tried to follow the steps outlined in them. Our expectations were still pretty low that the child would be a girl. We desired above all for this life to be healthy. Jeff had colic for the first eighteen months, which was hard for us to deal with at times. We both felt helpless, as he would double-up in stomach pain. I could often be seen with my arm held against his little tummy, as it seemed to tighten up. We wanted to take his pain unto ourselves.

The due date was around the eleventh of September,

which fell on a Wednesday. I was convinced that the second child would come early so I scheduled the entire week as vacation. I was going to be even more prepared this time, if that was possible. Today, we might have desired to know the child's gender, but I don't recall it as a possibility in 1974. We had attended the YMCA classes on prenatal care. I was ready for the moment. Unfortunately, this child had different plans. The week went by with no contractions. Dottie was bigger this time and we knew the baby would be normal size.

It was Sunday evening and we were at my parent's apartment. I was to go back to work in a few hours. We were about ready to return to our home when Dottie informed me that her water had just broken. Suddenly it was panic time. Everything we needed was at our house and Dottie needed to change first. I argued that the hospital was minutes away compared to about twenty minutes to the house, but she insisted it would be okay. I was prepared for an entire week and when the moment had come, everything was in disarray. When it comes to things we cannot control, we still seem to try anyway. Life has a way of humbling us.

Despite my anxiety, we arrived at the hospital on time. I was excited to get washed and robed for the delivery room. I did not get to see my son's birth and this might be my last chance to witness a miracle. We were now in the delivery room, ready for the moment. Dottie was pretty groggy from the pain medication. The doctor announced, "It's a girl." and I cannot put into words the tremendous joy that I felt. I remember raising Dottie's head so she could look into the mirror placed over the birthing area. "We got our girl." I cried and I think anyone within fifty miles could have heard me. I probably gave my wife a loss of hearing as well. The birth of my son was one defining moment and this certainly was another. We named her Tricia. I think it didn't really sink in for Dottie for a day or two, due to the medication. Our joy was complete.

PHILIPPIANS 4: 4 - 9 (NIV)

Rejoice in the Lord always. I will say it again: Rejoice! Let your gentleness be evident to all. The Lord is near. Do not be anxious about anything, but in everything, by prayer and petition, with thanksgiving, present your requests to God. And the peace of God, which transcends all understanding, will guard your hearts and minds in Christ Jesus.

A SPIRITUAL REALIZATION

The birth of our children went well beyond anything I could have imagined. I was now responsible for two young lives in all areas of their nurturing. Being a father is a tremendous experience, but it also carries awesome responsibility. I was providing for their physical needs, but what about their emotional and spiritual ones. I did not feel comfortable with my own emotions and I was a new Christian.

We had been attending the church where Dottie attended before our marriage, except in a new building. Before we left Michigan they had undertaken a fund-raising program and built a larger facility about a mile away from the old church. I felt obligated to return there due to Pastor Gale's untimely death during our honeymoon. I felt a strange spiritual tug inside ever since. I was twenty-five when I asked Jesus into my heart. Tricia had not yet been conceived and my responsibilities as a father had a big influence on that decision. I remember praying almost daily for help. I did not want to let my family down, especially my children.

I had always felt that I had a guardian angel watching over me. There were times when things that should have occurred, which would have been harmful, didn't happen. I felt like my angel was leading me when I first met Dottie. It was as if someone was saying that she is the one for me so forget about the girl from Illinois. I could not cite all of the incidents that made me feel as I did, but the feelings were real and often sustained me through tough times. My emotional pain was still buried deep inside from childhood, and when portions of it would surface, so would some form of spiritual peace. *Things will be okay,* seemed to be the message.

By now we had moved to our second home. It was much larger with a family room and in a good neighborhood. Our first home was like a small dollhouse with a small yard and in a poor neighborhood. The schools in our new area were much better for the needs of our family. Jeff had now started riding the school bus and Tricia was seen attempting to join him, wearing only a diaper. Her brother was her hero. She would follow him everywhere.

It was Easter or Mother's Day and I wanted my dad's mom to come and spend the night with us. I think Dad still harbored some negative feelings toward his mother, but we enjoyed spending time with her. Even at eighty years of age she had remarkable skills. Each of our children received a homemade quilt from her and she was hard to beat at *Scrabble.* Anyway, I was across town at her home when the phone rang. It was Dottie calling about an event involving Tricia. The words were chilling: "Your daughter has just been hit by a car. Don't worry." Then she hung up rather abruptly. I was an instant wreck. My emotions were on overload as I hurriedly placed grandma in the car. I had prayed frequently that if something happened to me, then my children would be cared for. Now my thoughts turned to my daughter.

I drove at a rapid rate across town to our house. It was normally a half hour drive and I think I did it in less than twenty minutes. No one was home so I began to call the doctor's office. Dottie was not there so I left word to call me if she arrived. Then I called the hospital with the same results. It was only a fifteen-minute drive to the office, which was close to the hospital. "Where could they be?" I was beginning to be a nervous wreck when the phone rang. Dottie was calling from the doctor's office and I could hear Tricia laughing in the background. A child's laughter is like a fingerprint. Her laugh had a unique quality and I would recognize it anywhere. My heart was instantly calmed as I sensed it was not as bad as I had imagined.

The incident changed my spiritual life. I would consider it another defining moment. Our neighbor had company from Canada staying with them. He had them park their car on the side of his driveway towards our house. He was backing out of the garage and was paying special attention to his guests when he felt something like a *thud*. He stopped the car and looked to his wife, who was looking out their kitchen window. She shouted, "Don't move!" and then ran outside. Tricia had wandered behind the guest's vehicle. She was two years old and was pulled out from under the passenger's rear wheel well of the neighbor's car.

I reviewed the incident over and over. I looked out the neighbor's kitchen window. And could not see anything behind the rear area of their car where Tricia was found. Then I wondered how she even got inside the wheel well when his car was in motion. There were no broken bones, only a few minor scrapes and soot. It could only be seen as a miracle. My neighbor's wife was able to see what was impossible to see, and reacted with the only advice that would not cause further harm: "Don't move." My prayer had been answered and God was watching over my family. I have not prayed that prayer since and I know God has great things planned for our daughter. Somehow, I believed that my mother was my guardian angel then. I thought that, perhaps, she was tired of my repetition and desired for me to get an answer to my prayer once and for all.

Years later Dottie and I would be at a Marriage Encounter. I remember discussing the lost time regarding this incident, when I arrived at our home and she had not yet reached the doctor's office. It had bothered me, but I had not understood what really happened until the encounter. At two in the morning, Dottie shared that she took the time to give Tricia a bath before taking her to the doctor's. I could understand why she hadn't shared that before as she probably felt I would somehow explode. I think I may have lost it if I was there at the time. To me her health would take precedence over her appearance. I'm sure Dottie would have done just that if she felt it was critical, but she didn't. She probably would have gone straight to the hospital in that case. The doctor's office was more of a precaution. After consideration of the event and the foreknowledge that everything was okay, we laughed together. It was the highlight for me of that encounter weekend.

I learned a lot from Grandma about my mother. I know that we boys got our receding foreheads from her side of the family. Mom's brothers were all bald on top and Dad's brothers all had a full head of hair until they died. I also learned for the first time from Grandma that Mom accepted Christ before she died, which has been described earlier. The timing was right for me as it put into perspective some of the things I was feeling about my guardian angel. My spiritual journey was now well on its way.

The responsibilities of child rearing still held me captive. I looked for opportunities to improve in that area and didn't feel like I was where I should be. Dave told me about a seminar that he had attended in Florida called The Bill Gothard Seminar. It was an intense forty-hour weeklong event. Monday through Friday covered about thirty hours with evening sessions along with a ten-hour Saturday. It included a textbook, a workbook, and videos. I learned a great deal about my role as a father and how we are to get under the umbrella of authority. I was to be the authority for my family like Christ is that for us. It was a concept that I have tried to apply ever since, even though it is difficult at times. I would recommend the seminar for anyone, especially my son.

RUMBLING EMOTIONS

The Marriage Encounter weekend had other significance for me as I was wrestling with feelings of separation from my wife. I suggested the encounter as a way to get the emotional closure that I thought I needed. Raising children had become a full time responsibility, leaving very little time for husband and wife communication except where it concerned the kids. We both loved our children and wanted to be good parents, but inside I felt that we needed to develop more as a couple. I desired for there to be an *us*. I thought that we could be much better in all our endeavors, including parenthood, if we also had our time together apart from the children. The encounter was two nights alone as husband and wife and not parents. Time together and alone was rare for us and I longed for it. I would feel more and more separated from Dottie when any suggestions that I made to be alone were often denied in favor of the children.

The first night we were asked to write down our personal answers to various questions. The first one was "Name three things that first attracted you to your spouse?" I was done very quickly as I wrote about her physical beauty, kind spirit, and beautiful eyes. Several minutes later the facilitator began to review our answers. Dottie had only written one thing on her paper, namely my generosity. She didn't realize it at the time, but it had a profound impact on me and would cause great unrest long into the future. I think I anticipated something about my physical appearance, my concerns for others or perhaps my sense of humor. It seemed very odd that my generosity was what had the most significance for her the day we met. I may have paid for the bowling or bought refreshments. Generosity has always been one of my traits, but somehow, as the only quality on her paper, I felt strange. "Was our relationship based on the things that I could provide?" It definitely struck an emotional chord and I desired to pursue it further.

I learned through our conversation that evening that her two-year on-and-off relationship with her last boyfriend was very different in the area of generosity. He was controlling and manipulating when it came to financial issues. Often they would go Dutch or she would have to pay for both of them. They discussed marriage and he told her that her car would have to go when that happened. If she worked, then her income would go to him and he would control it. I could easily see how my generous spirit was a welcome relief to her.

In addition, she grew up in a lower-class family. They had one car and Dad was the only driver. Mom would have to hoard any extra money that came her way, as she knew he would simply take it for himself. New things for her would be rare, yet he would replace the car quite frequently. It probably seemed so unfair for Dottie to see what her mother was going through and it heightened her appreciation for the quality of generosity when she would marry. I still couldn't help but wonder why she would still pursue her old boyfriend each time they would split up. She seemed to still want him despite his lack of passion for her. I understood why she would answer the question with my generosity as my number one quality, but it was the only answer. Her old boyfriend didn't have that as one of his traits and she still pursued him with vigor.

Whenever I felt emotionally separated, this event seemed to leap to the forefront of my mind. I would ask a question like "Am I needed just for the things I can provide?" It would make me feel so used and even further isolated in our marriage. My emotions would either create such a frustration inside that I would verbally explode or I would go to a quiet place and bawl like a baby. I was either a volcano erupting or a dam releasing its floodgates. Either way I was an emotional wreck. I truly loved my wife then and even more today. Perhaps it would have been easier to deal with if I didn't love her.

My childhood was without love and affection after the age of three, but I believe the first three years built a foundation that saw these things as necessities for happiness. Our long distance romance was filled with these things in the letter writing and due to the infrequency of actual contact; these areas were met when together. Affection in the form of touching was like an immediate release of all my anxieties. I would feel loved as never before and accepted as a man. When I was particularly feeling down I would even ask for a hug. Often even those requests were denied and my emotions would suffer.

Dottie's Mom and Dad were not openly affectionate. They were married, had children late in life and seemed to be of the school that taught to not display emotions in front of the children. I think the fact that I experienced it early in life would cause me to desire it all my life as it simply felt so good. I also believe that since Dottie may not have had the experience, she may have said to herself that she doesn't need it. For me it went deeper than that. I truly felt that due to the joy that I felt as a little boy when I was held, that it was an experience that I wished she could enjoy as well. I tried to tell myself that because she didn't need it, then neither should I, but it just didn't work.

In 1979, I was called up to the engineering department with the company. It was a huge step and leap of faith. I would be the new electrical technician working with engineers. I felt overwhelmed and challenged at the same time. My work record was reviewed and I was called up based on my qualifications. They believed in me and I was not going to let them down. Still, I felt that I would have to work hard and continue my night school classes to get my degree. I remember coming home one night after a mentally exhausting day. Dottie was making supper and it smelled wonderful. I commented on the aroma and how great she looked. Then I put my arms around her as she faced away working over the sink. I wished that she could feel the joy that I felt by just holding her, but she responded with words like, "How can you say I look beautiful. I am wearing jeans, my hair is a mess..." I let go in a hurry, apologized for being insensitive, and left, waiting for her to say dinner was ready. It was another emotional blow.

I let the incident go for a day or so and then came home from work asking to be greeted with a kiss or a hug, simply because I needed it as a break from work and home life. It would have taken a conscious effort on her part to meet my request, one that she was not willing to make. The emotional roller coaster seemed to be going more downhill than up. I can't explain everything about the human psyche when it comes to emotional trauma. I know my roller coaster would start surging upwards with just an occasional love tap, but somehow the deep hurts were still stored inside me. My highs were more like the moments when we do not feel pain any more even though we still have it. Sooner or later the medicine would wear off and the emotional discomfort would raise its head again. All I knew was that someday I wanted the pain to go away forever.

KEEPING COMMITMENTS

Dad taught each of his three sons to honor our commitments. When Mom died, he made a commitment to keep three boys together despite any hardship that it may have caused. His word was his bond and he honored his word. He may not have had a lot of money, but while we were growing up, we always knew we would have our summer fishing vacation. His second marriage was not without its problems, but Dad honored his vows until the day she died.

Three boys with the same experiences of losing a mother early in life and sharing foster homes together could have turned out quite different. We could have rebelled and decided to just live for ourselves. After all, few seemed to care about us. But, instead we sought to honor Mom and Dad with our schoolwork and when the time came we sought a family to grow old with. Each of us has kept our commitment to one woman and in the twenty-first century that is an accomplishment. We have been blessed with children of our own to nurture. They have blessed us with our treasured grandchildren. Dad was very proud of his sons.

Perhaps we didn't recognize that the suffering and grief that we understood as a child was part of our character building as adults. Each of us has developed a faith in God that may have been part of answered prayer by our mother before she died. We had to face the emotional demons as well and we persevered. Our trials are not over, but we continue to press forward with the hope that is in us. Along the way I feel a guardian angel still directing each of our paths.

I have learned, that like my father, I have a low tolerance for people who do not honor their commitments. If I tell someone that I will be there, they do not doubt that I will come. It actually grieves me if something totally unforeseen comes up that would cause me to have to break the vow. Yet, others who break commitments have let me down many times and it is very hard for me to believe them in the future. I am like my dad and desire for my word to be my bond.

Why do I toss in a chapter on commitments? It may seem like it is out of place, but to me it is not. When things were going suddenly awry early in my marriage and emotionally I felt separated, I did not desire to make it a permanent separation. I was committed to my marriage vows. I felt committed even more due to the tragedy of Pastor Gale's untimely passing. I did not desire someone else to give me comfort. I stayed committed to the welfare of my children. I strongly believe that people today make wedding vows with loopholes. The words: "If things don't work out, then I will get a divorce" seems to be commonplace by the over fifty percent divorce rate in America.

At this point Dottie and I had been married thirty years. We shared daily the joy in the lives of our grandchildren. I could not imagine what that would have been like if we had separated along the way. We still had our struggles, but I felt closer to her more then than I ever had and I can only imagine the trend continuing into the future. We have seen our children graduate from high school. We stayed committed to them through the college years. Each of their weddings was a proud moment that we shared together. We are now more aware of our personal hurts and desires and committed to each other to resolve them. The love we have for each other is forever.

Commitment took one more turn in our lives, which began in 1998. Dad was now living alone in his apartment in Merritt Island, Florida. The mother we knew had passed away several years earlier. I remember Dad telling me after she died, "I had to bathe her, cook her meals, clean up after her, get her pills…" as she was legally blind. "She was a lot of work." Then he paused, looked at her bed and said, "But if she wants to return, it's okay with me." To me that was a heartfelt commitment. He continued to play bridge several times a week, which he always enjoyed. He especially liked it when I would come down and play. As his partner, we did well, but at times he would pair me up with another, because he didn't want to break a previous date, and my new partner and I would go on and win against him. Dad didn't seem to mind, even though he held the highest honor in the game. He was a life master, which took years of commitment to achieve. He always took pride in the accomplishments of his sons, even if he didn't express it in ways we would understand. We would talk after the match and discuss the playing of the bridge hands.

On one occasion I was his partner and made an opening bid that indicated a relatively weak hand. The opponents made a strong bid and dad attempted to interfere in their bidding by raising my bid above what he thought we could make. This was called a sacrifice, as we would keep them out of making an even better game bid. The other opponent passed as dad expected and then I paused to reflect the bidding sequence. I then raised my suit to an even higher level, where if we made it, we would score over a thousand points instead of a few hundred. The opponents did not think I would make such a bid so they doubled, which adds considerable penalty for not making the bid. In the game of bridge only one player bidding plays the cards while reviewing his partner's cards face up on the table. Dad as my partner had to lay down his cards. I remember how upset he looked at my bid, as if to say that I shouldn't have made it. Then I remember the look of awe as I proceeded to actually make the bid. We took high hand on that one with no one even close and his pride began to radiate all over his face. That was his son in whom he was well pleased. Then we got word that they found him unconscious in his apartment and that he was in emergency.

Dad was eighty-seven years old at that point. He had kept his bitterness towards those whom he felt rejected him when he needed them. Now he had a stroke. He had missed a bridge date, which was very unusual. Two days later he missed another one and his bridge-playing friends knew something was wrong. They went to his apartment and after there was no answer, sought help from the superintendent. They found him lying near his nightstand with a cut on his head and no movement. It had been three days without his medicine for diabetes, no food, and no water. Because of commitments made to his bridge players he was found and he was alive.

When I arrived soon afterwards, Dad was conscious. He recognized me along with his other sons. His left side was very weak and he had difficulty swallowing. We knew he needed special care and placed him in a nursing home. Dave lived about two hundred miles away and would travel to see him as often as he could. Each time he would bring audiotapes and books for his soul. We desperately desired for Dad to have spiritual peace before he died and Dad's condition looked pretty grim.

About the same time I was contemplating an early retirement as the company was going through considerable downsizing. I did not enjoy my work as I used to, due to the new policies being made and wanted the change. I was only fifty and wanted to continue working, but felt that I would do better on the outside, letting my retirement rollover as an IRA. I would receive two years salary at half pay, so I would have time to build up a new career path. Perhaps, it was also a way to deal with the emotional pain that I knew was still there. I did very well the first year financially and reduced nearly all debt outside the mortgage payment, but I kept feeling the pull to go be with Dad. That would mean leaving my wife and family in New York. I had an offer to work for a friend who was located in Orlando, only forty-five minutes from Dad, which I finally took.

Dad had been in the nursing home for about nine months when I went down. Weekends, especially Sundays after church, were dedicated to being with him. We tried to play cards at first, but it was obvious that he no longer understood how to play. It was difficult, as he knew that is was something that he enjoyed. He would try to sort stamps for his collection without success. Dave and I bought a jumbo-print Bible for him to read as he was an avid reader, but he did not comprehend the meaning of the words. With the help of strong glasses he could see the letters and try to sound the words, but his recognition memory was now gone.

The stroke had taken away everything but his ability to recognize people, hear others, speak, and think. Everything that he had done to escape reality was gone, but somehow he was still able to reason. Dave and I had spoke about spiritual things and he would speak about winning the lottery and leaving that place. His rebellion was real.

After fourteen months I was at the point where my goal was to make him laugh sometime in my visit. He was now eighty-nine years old and hard to take him out even in a wheel chair. I knew that he still looked forward to my visits and we never located the winning lottery money that he said he won or the new Cadillac that he had bought. On this particular day I made a decision to be baptized and it was to happen at three in the afternoon. I picked Dad up, loaded him into the van, and then loaded his chair. I shared with him of my decision to be baptized and would have to leave by two in the afternoon instead of waiting until after suppertime. The jumbo-print Bible that we gave him was in the wheelchair, which was unusual. We had our late breakfast and I loaded him back in the van. I placed the Bible on his lap and then jumped in the driver's seat. It was one o'clock.

I asked him if he had been reading the Bible and he answered that he tried. Then I asked him if there was something that he didn't understand that I could help him with. He answered, "All I know is that I want to go to heaven as I think that is where my boys are going to be." My heart seemed to leap out of my body with excitement. I asked him if he knew how to get to heaven and he said, "No." Then I proceeded with a question like: "Do you understand that you are a sinner." He answered, "I didn't do anything wrong." Then I asked him if he ever held a grudge along with a few other hot buttons and he answered, "Oh *yes*." Then I said, "If you were the Creator of everything including heaven, would you want someone like you to come inside. He answered sheepishly, "Oh *no*." Then I spoke about Jesus taking our sins away on the cross so that we could enter. I shared the steps to salvation and he made the prayers. I was so moved by his sincerity and I could feel the scales of bitterness falling off. I asked him who he would see in heaven when he got there and without hesitation he said, "Your mom." My guardian angel was there for Dad as well.

Was it my decision to be baptized on that day, which touched his heart? Was it the fact that I told him before we had our late breakfast, giving him time to reflect on my words at the table? Could it have been something that he was considering after all the council received from David and I? He had time to reflect. That was what God had left him after the stroke. Whatever the reason, my dad had made the most exciting and eternal decision that he could ever have made.

The trip back was nothing less than euphoric. I was on cloud nine. I called Dottie and could hardly speak two words without crying tears of joy. She sensed my joy and for a moment we emotionally bonded. It was another defining moment for me. Then I called Dave as I always shared my visits with Dad after I would leave him. I was so caught up in the moment that I missed my turn and was almost late for my baptism. The pastor who had talked to me about being baptized made a statement that was profound to me. He said, "Why do you want to withhold God's blessings for your life?" He believed that the act of baptism was more than an outward confession to God, but an event where God was ready to pour out an extra measure of goodness for being faithful. When I arrived at the site, I told the pastor that I had already received my reward.

I wrote two accounts in the jumbo-print Bible that Dad had on that day. One was for the day that I committed myself to God in baptism and the other for the day that Dad received salvation. A few weeks passed and I found myself asking the question: "How could an eighty-nine-year-old man understand the commitment that he had made?" I asked God for a sign. It was on a Friday. The following Sunday I made my weekly visit. When I signed him out I noticed that Dave had signed him out on that Friday and I remember wondering why he would come up without calling me. After my visit I called Dave and asked him that question. He said that he had the day off and decided to just come up. He figured that I was busy and didn't want to bother me. Then he said something that caught my curiosity. He said Dad was singing in the car. It was odd because we had never heard Dad sing before. Then he continued, "It was not the fact that he was singing, but rather what he was singing." Now I was more than curious. He was singing, "When the Roll is Called Up Yonder." In an instant God had once again answered my prayer and I knew Dad was going to heaven.

Dad did not reach his ninetieth birthday. During the days and weeks prior, he was in obvious pain and it was hard to see him that way. When I heard the news, I rejoiced. Dad was with Jesus. No more pain or sorrow. Dave was choked up when he heard the news. As he pulled out of his street he heard a song come across the radio that soothed his heart. It was titled: "If You Could See Me Now" which talks about being in heaven. We conducted Dad's funeral with those hymns as our backdrop. We spoke about our dad being in heaven and not about his death.

There were two non-relatives there that day listening to words of joy and were moved to tears. They spoke with Dave and I afterwards. One was Dad's superintendent, who went to a Catholic church where Dad lived. He said that he never heard words like those we spoke and we opened the Bible to him. Then the woman who played the music came forward with tears streaming from her eyes. She said, "I have been doing the music for this funeral hall for over nine years and I never have been so moved like this." I looked up and silently said a prayer to heaven that was meant for Dad. It went like: "Dad, you have only been gone a short while and already you have touched two people." I remember smiling as I could picture Mom and Dad together forever.

THE REUNION

It is now time to reflect. Mom and Dad are with the Lord. We have a residence in Oviedo, Florida, and another one in Rochester, New York. Dottie has been traveling down to Florida, but prefers to be near our family in New York. My work takes me throughout the state, at times, so Dottie's trips can also leave her somewhat isolated. Her best friend, Jan, is about three and a half miles farther south in Florida. My job pays well and is enjoyable. The thought of retirement at fifty-five is an option, but not a very attractive one. Therefore, we decided to just keep going for a time to see what better options unfold.

During the events that led Dad to the Lord, prayers were being answered almost routinely. In one case a need was met even without asking. When I started working for my friend in Orlando, I was driving a two-door coupe, which required stretchable tie down cords to hold the trunk lid, when Dad's wheelchair was loaded. I remember thinking about trading for a used van or SUV, that would make it easier to get Dad in and out as well as the wheelchair. Shortly after having that thought, I received a call from a large corporation asking me if I could talk. The conversation was about a new job position requiring someone with my work experience living in the central Florida area to assist sales for the company's product lines. A manager and sales team met with me shortly afterwards to discuss the position. Even though the product line was new to me, they were willing to provide the training necessary. Because the work would take me throughout the state, a company car was also part of the package. It would have been difficult to say no to a substantial increase in salary plus a vehicle; however, the icing on the cake came when they asked me if I would prefer a van. I think the sound of my jaw dropping could have been heard for miles.

I only worked eight months with my friend before taking on the new responsibility. I had a small apartment close to the office. The new job did not have restrictions as to where to live, but the primary salesman was on the east side of town. I began to look for a home near where he lived with easy access to major arteries that would allow me to travel throughout the state. This process also worked as a blessing for my previous employer, who wanted to drop the product line that I was supporting. My work with him was bringing in revenue, but the company supplying the products was requiring costly mandates, that would take years to recover. Later, I learned that my new employer received my name from my previous employer's brother. As a result, new doors of opportunity were suddenly opened.

One of these doors involved training. Since I needed to quickly learn the new products, I began to develop training aids for my use. Each one focused on a specific topic using

Microsoft Word® or PowerPoint®. I would assemble them in logical order in binders for quick reference and then when a specific subject came up with a client, I would hand them just that section. The corporate center for training was in Atlanta, Georgia. During management reviews I would show them my training materials, which would then get passed on to the head of training. To help my new customers fully understand the power of the software used with the products, I wrote a "Jump Start" manual. This was designed to open the eyes of potential customers in a four-hour seminar. Six seminars were then scheduled in the Atlanta area over a three-day period, followed by a meeting with corporate managers including the Training department. The materials were very well received but the training manager felt that it would reduce enrollment for training. Corporate management felt differently and the materials that I was developing for my use in Florida began to change the way the course offerings for the company would be handled. This would have great significance later as you will see.

The company, that I was now employed with, seemed to be well pleased with my role as application engineer in Florida. Prior to my hiring, resources had to be pulled from the Atlanta area. Sales leads for the state could now be handled quickly and training new customers on the company product lines was a key part. Growth in the southeast for the company exceeded expectations for several years. My job was rewarding and I hoped it would carry me until my wife and I decided to retire, perhaps as early as when I turned fifty-nine and one half, but at least by age sixty-two. Nevertheless, I longed for my wife to spend more time with me in Florida.

Several times I questioned whether to just quit working and move back to Rochester to be with Dottie full time. Each time I had the thought a new thought would take its place. I felt as if God wanted me right where I was. I told the Lord that I would wait on His direction. One day in 2002, about a year after Dad had passed, I was in the training department in Atlanta. I stopped by to see the manager and his secretary said he was out looking to hire a new trainer. I told her that training would be a good final career path for me and that my name should be considered in the future. His secretary told me to submit a request. About three weeks later, while I was back in Florida, I sent an e-mail to the manager asking to be considered as a trainer in Atlanta. I enjoyed writing course materials and instructing. Best of all, it would minimize my traveling, allowing some normalcy for Dottie when she visited. The manager called me the following morning with joy in his voice. As soon as an opening occurs, I would have it.

God was not done with us yet. The opening for a trainer seemed to be delayed. Then I received an email from our daughter that brought tears to my eyes. She wanted to be a stay-at-home mom. Her job as a special education teacher in New York State paid more than her husband's job and carried all the benefits. Her husband was seeking new employment with higher pay and benefits in New York, but had no success. The search had started to take them out of New York State via the Internet. My daughter said the search had taken them to the Atlanta area. Tears of joy streamed down my face. Little did she know that I had thrown my hat into the ring as a trainer there as well.

The thought of having my daughter's family there with me triggered many possibilities. Surely Dottie would want to move out of Rochester when her daughter was no longer there. Two of our three grandchildren would be in Atlanta. We would combine the sale of two houses into one, which Dottie could help find while was still working in Florida. I would have family, still be employed, and be able to schedule things to do together without the problems of traveling. Perhaps, Dottie and I could have a "Date Night" on a regular basis to help rekindle emotions and resolve any conflicts.

Our daughter and her family made the move to Auburn, Georgia (about thirty-five miles northeast of Atlanta), in the spring of 2004. As expected, Dottie spent many weeks helping with the move, decorations, and of course watching our grandchildren. The fall of 2004 would bring me to the training department, when an opening finally occurred. By that time Dottie was ready to relocate. She found a home about seven miles from our daughter in a town called Dacula. The house was bigger than either house we owned, with a full basement. The move would begin with the sale of our home in Florida. The Florida market was booming, so I had a good down payment to use towards the home in Dacula. The loan would allow me to apply a lump sum payment to further reduce the payment when the house in New York was sold. That would happen in early 2005. The unity of our family would be complete. We would still have ties in New York to bring us back there, but home was now in Georgia.

The possessions from Florida would be small in comparison to those from New York. My efforts to furnish the home there were second-rate in comparison to the great attention to detail by Dottie in New York. She is the far better coordinator and decorator. I took pride in saving money at the local yard sales. Dottie would once again have the role of decorator, which was a role that I enjoyed for her. Our daughter would help, which Dottie welcomed with joy. By the time both house contents were brought into the new house, we were glad that we had a huge basement. We also had a bonus room above the two-car garage, which became part office and mostly a grandchildren's getaway.

The hardest part was leaving our son, Jeff, who resides in Rochester. First his sister left and now Mom. Keeping the house in Rochester was discussed at length, but not very practical. The home Jeff knew since 1978 was no longer in the family. I'm sure the memories made the move difficult. Jeff told us that he was okay with the move and that home was where the heart is anyway. We had his blessing and best of all Mom and Dad are together.

REVELATION 14:17 (NIV)

Blessed are those who die in the Lord... they are blessed indeed, for they will rest from all their toils and trials; for their good deeds follow them.

A NEW BATTLE

We are now enjoying each other's presence in our new home in Georgia. My role as a technical instructor was challenging and rewarding. My work with customers in Florida allowed me to develop new course offerings, based on my customer's needs. The work was not only fruitful, but also enjoyable. The drive to work was about twenty-five miles each way, but living near our daughter made the trip much easier. At least I would not have to drive around the state.

Each year, usually in the spring, we would attend a weeklong training event to brush up on old skills as well as become familiar with new ones. Events like these allowed me to reunite with the application engineers, whom I was associated with during my years in Florida. The spring of 2005 would have a reversal of roles for me. Instead of taking courses, I would be teaching them. However, there were occasions when I would present teaching materials to my engineer peers at these events. Anyway, on this occasion I developed two new course offerings, which took one and a half days each. Near the end of the first session I received a call from my wife that would send me reeling.

We spent Easter Sunday at our daughter's house, including a wonderful ham dinner. Dottie felt a pain in her stomach, which she thought was from overeating. The pain stayed with her all the next day as well. On Tuesday she decided to make an appointment with the doctor. Her doctor touched the area where the pain seemed to be the worst and felt a mass. He immediately sent her to the hospital for a CT scan to get more definition. When my wife made the call while I was finishing up the training session, I heard the word *cancer* and cringed.

A series of tests were done to try and isolate where the cancer started, which would help identify the best treatment. Many cancer trials are also available for specific cancers like lung or colon. A small percentage of cancers, less than five percent, are called unknown primary or adenocarcinoma where the cancer starts at one location and then migrates to other areas. Dottie was in this category. This would pose a problem for her oncologist who would make decisions on the method of treatment. All we were told was that it was glandular, with the probable areas being pancreas, gall bladder, colon, bile duct, kidney, or liver. One thing for sure is that my family would now learn all we could, using the Internet to help in the process. Our daughter took on the role as medical secretary. Dottie was not going to go through this alone.

Surely, God did not bring us back together to face this? My initial thoughts and feelings seemed to question God's motives, yet I was comforted by the fact that at least we were together. Having to deal with cancer while we were living

1,200 miles apart would have been unbearable and I would have certainly made different choices. There was no cancer in Dottie's family. She ate healthy, exercised and was the one I would least expect as a candidate. My mother died from cancer. My dad had stomach cancer in his early eighties, which he seemed to beat with chemotherapy. If anyone was to have cancer in my family, it should have been me. The next several months would have me second-guessing God with a barrage of *why* questions. It just did not make sense. Somehow, I maintained my faith and trust in God, that everything would work out. We asked the doctor what his best guess might be for when the cancer started and he said five or six years ago. That would have put it around the time when I left New York to minister to Dad in the nursing home. The thought was not very comforting.

Dottie met with several doctors starting with an oncologist, who scheduled a biopsy of a ten-centimeter mass on her liver. The test would indicate cancer. The CT scan showed that the cancer had spread into her lungs and had a spot on her spine. The spinal area was addressed first to prevent Dottie from becoming paralyzed. A radiologist was called in who performed radiation on the eleventh vertebra. The treatments covered approximately three weeks. The results appeared to be successful. Follow up tests weeks later would confirm the lack of new activity at the spinal cord site. These treatments were once-a-day walk-in low doses of radiation, where Dottie was able to handle without support.

The next phase involved chemotherapy, administered by the oncologist. Side effects like nausea and hair loss were discussed. There was medicine to minimize nausea and wigs for hair loss. We figured we could handle the side effects. Dottie listened to her doctor's advice and was willing to follow whatever he said. Other tests were ordered to help isolate the initial cause like a colonoscopy, which showed no cancer. The oncologist started Dottie on a chemo mixture that was effective for bile duct cancer. She would go to the doctor's office for Gemzar through an IV once a week and take Tarceva in pill form daily for two weeks. Then she would get a week off. The process would continue for six weeks. One side effect of the Tarceva was sores in Dottie's mouth. These sores were not only painful, but they made swallowing difficult. Dottie was susceptible to bloody noses during the chemo and needed an ear nose and throat specialist. After the six-week period a new CT scan was ordered, which indicated an increase in size of the cancer areas. The lung spots no longer showed activity, however. Another six-week session was tried without change and then a new option needed to be tried.

The next chemo option required Dottie to get a port implanted. She would get an IV at the doctor's office and then take home a pump that she would wear for the next two days. Two milliliters per hour of the chemo would be slowly pumped through the port. This would repeat every three weeks. Dottie would also take pills for ten days after the pump. The week without chemo was good for shopping with the girls as Dottie gained well-needed strength. Although the first CT scan looked promising, the next one revealed that the chemo combination was not being effective again. This time Dottie lost her hair. The chemo used was Taxol, Carboplatin, and VP16. Since the size of the cancer areas seemed to be stable, Dottie took about six months off.

In July 2006, the doctor wanted Dottie to consider one more chemo option using a new drug called Avastin, which had shown to be very effective against several cancers. Avastin was a very expensive option and because Dottie's origin was unknown, insurance would not cover it. The doctor contacted the drug company and an agreement was made so Dottie could try it. Again the pump would be used after an initial IV. Each week's treatment was a guessing game due to low platelet counts. Dottie would end up with the Avastin only three times over a four-month period. An initial decrease in size of the mass on her liver gave hope, but then the mass began to grow again.

It looked like chemotherapy had nothing left to offer. In January 2007 we told that the options available to her doctor were exhausted. He gave us three studies to review, of which two were not possible, because Dottie already had the drug involved. The third involved a clinic in Houston, Texas. This one involved a study of the cancer gene. The study most likely would not be covered by any medical insurance. Dottie needed to get her counts up so for the next month she took a break from treatment.

On February 2, I was leaving work to meet my wife, daughter, and her family at a nearby bowling alley. When I arrived everyone was done bowling and just waiting for me. Dottie had only bowled a few frames when she felt sick to her stomach. She went to the ladies room and noticed that her vomit looked like blood. She called our daughter who agreed. By the time I arrived, the discussion was to get Dottie to a hospital. Within seconds Dottie felt sick again. This time I saw the deep purple-colored vomit and it was over a pint. I took her to the hospital's emergency department. By the time she was called they tested her stomach for blood and it was clear. She was released around midnight and I took her home. At five a.m. I was awakened by the sound of vomiting. The picture of bright red blood in the toilet and diarrhea triggered an immediate call to 911. By the time the ambulance arrived, Dottie was cleaned up and ready for a trip back to the hospital. Her blood pressure was 70/40 and later dropped to 32/20 in emergency. I thought I had lost her. She needed four units of blood. Miraculously, she recovered. The blood came from a lacerated esophagus near where it attached to the stomach. Several agonizing days later and she was released. The hardest part of this account was that Dottie could not have fluids by mouth until the laceration was healed. Ice chips were a delicacy.

The clinic option became our last hope for a cure. Dottie's medical records were sent to the clinic and she was accepted as a new patient. We visited the clinic to get information and the expected costs. Our home was refinanced to get the cash out and we made a second trip to Houston. The clinic's typical client was at stage IV and yet their positive response rate was much higher than what we heard from the oncologist. Everything sounded optimistic so Dottie started the process, which would slowly acquaint Dottie's body with a liquid oral medicine. The doses started at five milliliters and would work up to thirty milliliters six times a day. The first three days seemed to be going well. By the fourth day Dottie was losing energy. I would have to wake her up to take her medicine. On the fifth day she only two doses and I made the decision to let her rest. The next day she was too weak to even walk so I carried her to our car and drove to the clinic, where she was given an IV. The doctor on call called for an ambulance to take her to a hospital nearby. There she was diagnosed with Klubsuela pneumonia, which is an extremely dangerous bacterial form. She would stay there for another nine days. Our daughter and son would fly out to be with her. Again we thought we would lose her there, but she pulled through. Miraculously, Dottie was able to travel home by car needing an additional week of antibiotics.

For a time she was able to do the things she enjoyed, especially with the grandchildren. Her quality of life was a far improvement over the last several weeks. Maintaining some equilibrium in her electrolytes was difficult. Her sodium levels were usually below the lower limit of 135, but she would start shaking when it neared 125. We had started a rigorous dietary supplement approach that included pills and medicine from the clinic and concentrated levels of fruits and vegetables. Her pillbox contained twenty-eight compartments so we could monitor each day's intake. Dottie was determined to take her pills. In addition Dottie would take a special tea brew that worked well for several cancers. Our daughter had printed out daily medicine reminders so we could log everything.

On April 30 our daughter stayed with Dottie while I attended church service. At the end of the service I received a call from our daughter stating that she took mom to the hospital due to weakness and shaking. They gave her an IV and told us to contact her oncologist. The doctor examined Dottie the next day and admitted her for low sodium with elevated calcium. She would remain in the hospital for a week. The outlook was not good and we asked about hospice support. He said that now would be the time. Fluid buildup on her abdomen and legs was worsening. Prior to leaving the hospital the doctor ordered a draining of the area, which removed four and one half liters of fluid. Hospice had dropped off some equipment, including oxygen, an airbed, wheelchair, and a potty chair. Dottie wanted to lay down on either her living room couch or on her bed. The last thing Dottie wanted to see again was a hospital bed. Therefore, the airbed would only take up space. Our bedroom was rearranged to allow easier access to the bathroom.

During the next few weeks we had twenty-four-hour family support at the house. Dottie's lifelong friend and sister-in-law, Jan, would offer her nursing skills to give me some relief and care for her friend. Other friends would come to stay with Dottie to allow family to have a reprieve. Our son would take more time off to spend time with his mom. Hospice services would be minimal. Dottie's family made the time at home the best we could with soft music, the smell of lilacs, and family pictures. Each day we would help her to the couch she loved, as friends would stop by to say hello. If the Lord was not going to cure her, then my prayer was for her to see everyone that she desired and not be in pain. Due to her discomfort, we started Dottie on the lowest dosage of morphine. This dosage was later increased until she was comfortable. Several friends from Rochester, New York, stopped by and Dottie was noticeably joyous.

On the night of May 31, I was prepared to dispense the normal amount of morphine throughout the night, yet Dottie slept calmly and peacefully. At seven the next morning I woke Jan to help me turn Dottie to her other side. I asked about the morphine. Since Dottie was in no pain it was not necessary. Around noon, Dottie's breathing began to accelerate from a breath every eight seconds to nearly one per second. Jan told me to call our daughter, as she knew Dottie's time was at hand. At 1:50 that afternoon Dottie went peacefully to be with her Lord.

From the first day, when Dottie learned of her cancer, she trusted her Savior. If the Lord wanted to heal her, the doctors would provide the remedy. Dottie was quick to let everyone know that she would be okay. She met several cancer survivors who gave her hope and at the same time was an inspiration to everyone she met. Through the battle Dottie never stopped caring for the needs of others and maintained her strong faith in Jesus Christ as Lord of her life. Cancer laid claim to her earthly body, but it had no power over her soul. Her legacy of love lives on in the hearts of all who knew her.

EPHESIANS 2:10 (NIV)

For we are God's workmanship, created in Christ Jesus to do good works, which God prepared in advance for us to do.

GOD'S CALLING

Why Dottie? Why now at only sixty-two years of age? What do we do now?

These are typical questions when a loved one is lost. Often, we never get our answers. Sometimes, however, God uses these times to speak to us through others. Dottie's illness came after we were finally back together as husband and wife in one locale. Emotionally, things looked so much better. Our love for each other was never questioned and only grew stronger as we battled the cancer together. It was during this time when God called me to a ministry and gave me a new purpose for the rest of my life.

The calling actually started when I went to minister to Dad in the nursing home in 1998. I was torn between leaving my wife and family in New York and desiring to provide some joy to my dad in a depressing place. I tried to say no to going, but I felt an overwhelming urge to say yes. God was going to use me for His purposes and I heeded the call. My other brothers were not able to be there. My previous employer would still be paying my salary and I had an offer to work for a friend in the Orlando area. I may have felt that the time would be relatively short. After all, Dad was eighty-seven years old when he had the stroke. After Dad passed away I felt the need to share his story with my brothers and family so I wrote a manuscript called *A Legacy of Love*, which consisted of the first twelve chapters of this document.

I learned a great deal about my family origin from my father along the way that needed to be captured somehow for generations to follow. As a society, we are already forgetting the legacy left during World War II, by perhaps the greatest generation ever and Dad was a part of that. The world is even trying to say that the Holocaust never happened or that Hitler was not that big a threat. Christianity is under attack everywhere, especially in the United States. The words "Under God" in the Pledge of Allegiance—that we recited in schools as kids—is in danger of being removed. Other religions can pray any time or place they desire and we call it their right, but not Christians. The Ten Commandments is being removed from public places despite the fact that our laws were based on their premise. Dad had a story to tell that brought him from the foxholes in Germany to the outstretched arms of Jesus Christ. I sat down one Friday evening in our home in Florida and started writing.

You can only imagine how the words began to flow from a hunt-and-peck typist, but over seventy pages were written that weekend. It was as if God took control of the keyboard and let my fingers follow the bouncing keys. I had written a book while employed in New York, which took three days per chapter. Suddenly I had typed twelve chapters in the same time. I'm sure that my typing skills were not that much improved. In fact, someone else typed the first book for me from a penned manuscript. After several proof readings and edits, the manuscript was copied and bound for my family to have as a legacy.

Over the next several years, many people had told me that they would like a copy or that I should have it published. I denounced the publishing idea as it was about family and for family. I felt good about getting the story out and the process of writing was a new vocation for me. Writing was an outlet to express myself to my fiancé from the Air Force barracks for those twelve-hour duties. The time away from my family in New York also gave me time to write thoughts and feelings down without any fear of being hurt. Dottie would return her thoughts as well. Whenever I wanted to release frustration, I would just write. Dottie and I would communicate in letters and the process was therapeutic.

I remember one occasion when Dottie had called after receiving a letter. We talked for a time and then I could feel my frustration level rise. Prior to this frustration would cause me to elevate my vocal tones without realizing it. On this occasion my voice began to drop. I wanted to end the conversation to gather my thoughts and Dottie persisted that I talk it out. Then I shared that I felt like I was falling in a pit with nowhere to land. Something in my voice told her to let me hang up and she agreed to call back later. It was only minutes later and we discussed the incident. At that time I knew that she finally heard the little child crying out "Doesn't anybody love me?" or "Doesn't anybody care about me?" It was a defining moment for both of us. The loss of a mother when I was three left an emotional scar long into my adult life. The relationship Dottie and I had from that point on began my emotional closure. All of our married life I had placed the burden of relief on my wife and now I was beginning to get that relief. I think writing had a lot to do with that. I also believe that God wanted me to have the feelings that I had to share with others.

Once the legacy manuscript was written, I felt relief. I thought of returning to Rochester and just as quickly felt something more defining to keep me in Florida. It was as if God was saying, "You are right where I want you. Wait on me." I shared these feelings with Dottie and we agreed to persevere, besides, I was too young to retire from working. The events that led us to Georgia would then follow. I would count it a privilege to be used by God to lead Dad to salvation and that alone would justify the time in Florida. Now we were beginning a new life together in a new place. The bonus was that our daughter and two grandchildren would also be there.

I had picked out the house in Florida without Dottie seeing it (fortunately she approved). Now we had a reversal of roles and Dottie got to select the home in Georgia. She did let me see it first, however. We also met there to help our daughter find her home, so we were semi-accustomed to area by the time we moved. The move did involve two houses, however, and the stress of moving two households caused me to develop herpes, which manifested painful headaches and sores on the left side of my face. I understood the potential affects of stress. Little did I know at the time that the stress Dottie was feeling in New York at the time I left for Florida, might have triggered the cancer.

We were thrown for a loop when the cancer diagnosis came. I questioned God about the timing. I told Him that I wanted to return to New York earlier and was told to wait, like everything was in control. It made no sense to me that this would be part of what He was referring to. We were getting emotional closure and drawing closer than ever as husband and wife. Retirement was on the horizon, where we could enjoy just being with each other doing the things we both enjoyed. We would definitely be involved with our grandchildren's lives. Perhaps, God wanted us to draw closer because of the cancer. I would be there for Dottie. The resources we had would be used to find a cure. Losing Dottie to cancer was not on my mind initially. God wouldn't bring us together for that end.

I had a habit of chilling out in a local coffee shop. I would gather my thoughts about home and work as well as meet people along the way. The months to follow would keep me from traveling in my work as much as possible. I would attend Dottie's doctor visits, then let Dottie choose each new option. I was her biggest supporter along with our daughter. During this process the coffee shops would become a new source of information that would lead me to an unmistakable knowledge of what God wanted me to do with the rest of my life.

On Father's Day 2005, the church we were attending handed out a special gift to each father in the congregation. It was a book called *Half Time* by Bob Buford. I read the book in an afternoon and was deeply impressed. The book talked about how we lived the first part of our lives supporting our family (success) and the end part as our epitaph (significance). The second half would be slowly added while we were successfully raising our family. Then at some point we would no longer work our career and begin the new one of significance for God. In other words we would begin to leave His legacy. I was convinced after reading the book, that my second half involved writing. That was my new found passion. By this time I had written several manuscripts, two of which were based on scripture accounts. I enjoyed studying the Bible and capturing insights. Little would I know that this Father's Day gift would open my eyes to what God wanted for me to now do for Him.

On one coffee shop visit I met a man who had a large stack of typed papers next to the computer that he was using. I asked him if he was a writer. He answered yes and I acknowledged that I also liked to write. I shared the story of my dad that I gave to my family and he said I should seek publication of it. He said it had meaning for many others. The book he was writing was over a thousand pages in length about the Civil War and that he found a book on publishing that was the most helpful to lead him to the right agent for his work. He then pulled out a business card and wrote the name of the book on publishing on the back. I thanked him for the information and placed the card in my wallet. I did not take it any further. After all, the "Legacy of Love" manuscript was for my family. Who else would want to read it? Having it published was not on my mind. I did consider it for one of the other manuscripts that I wrote, however. Still his business card would be hidden away for a while.

Another coffee shop experience would lead to answered prayer. A group of men were discussing a Bible study on Romans. Stan was really getting a lot out of the study and seemed excited when he talked about it. I introduced myself and asked Stan if the study was open to others outside of his church. He invited me to the next study the following Wednesday morning at 6:30. It was at a restaurant also known for great coffee and on my way to the training department where I worked. I had been asking God to help me locate a men's fellowship, where I could have accountability partners, enjoy the fellowship and perhaps share a round of golf together. Stan was in real estate and we exchanged business cards. Stan introduced the men from his church at the restaurant on the following Wednesday. The men's church was only a few miles from where I lived.

The study was wonderful and the men were very open to my presence. They also became prayer partners for Dottie and I during the battle against cancer. During this time our four-year-old granddaughter was to be scheduled for open-heart surgery due to a hole in her heart discovered from birth. The doctors now thought it was time for the operation. My family had a lot going on and having a group of men to lean on was a tremendous blessing. After a short time an e-mail announcement was sent letting us know that the meeting date would be moved to Tuesdays for a couple of weeks, due to a conflict. Stan had come for a couple weeks, but his work had kept him away for the last few meetings.

On the first Tuesday meeting I met a new believer, who I did not see at the previous Wednesday meetings that I attended. His name was Rich and he was into investments. With a name like Rich, I found that somewhat amusing, but at the same time I was considering retirement so the handling of my investments was on my mind. I was nearing fifty-nine and a half years old. I could begin to use my IRA investments without the ten percent penalty assigned to younger owners. Along with exchanging business cards, Rich was sharing about the new church golf league that started that night. The course he mentioned was about three miles from my home. I asked if anyone could play since it was a private club. The price of twenty dollars per week seemed too good to be true; since guests paid over fifty dollars for eighteen holes and needed to be escorted by a member. Rich assured me that I should come out and play. It did not take any heavy arm-twisting to get my okay and I played that night. God had begun to answer my prayers in a big way.

During this time of fellowship I had to make plans for

Dottie's trip to Houston, which required refinancing our home to get cash out. I had stopped at our local bank on several occasions to meet with a mortgage counselor, but it seemed as though God had other plans. I remembered Stan was in the real estate business, and located his card. I called Stan to get a recommendation for a mortgage broker and he introduced Dottie and I to his wife, who was on a Christian finance commission associated with their church. We made the appointment with Stan's wife, Shannon, to get the refinance started. Not only did we get the money for the trip, but we also had a new prayer partner.

We came back from the Houston trip somewhat mystified. We felt the calling to go there, as it was the only option left from Dottie's oncologist. The bout with pneumonia was a real set back and now our priorities focused on trying to get Dottie some strength back. The thought of losing her in Texas was difficult. Now, back home and some relief may have been seen on the faces of family and friends. When Dottie went back into the hospital in early May to get her electrolytes back in balance, our granddaughter's surgery was also being scheduled. I had hoped that Dottie would have been out of the hospital before the open-heart surgery was to be performed, but God had still other plans. Kelly, our granddaughter, was admitted on Thursday and her surgery would begin early the next day. Dottie was nearing her release, but it would be delayed until Monday when her excessive fluids would be drained. I was torn since Kelly was in a children's hospital about forty minutes away. I couldn't be in two places at once. My place was with Dottie. Our son was also with us. The next several hours of waiting for updates from our daughter kept us on pins and needles. The news of Kelly's uneventful surgery was shear joy for Dottie, our son, and myself.

The following Monday seemed to let us know that God was there all the time. I was sitting with my son outside the operating room where Dottie was having the fluid drained. Stan called to see how things were with Dottie and shared another incident that brought out a stream of tears from my eyes. He said that Shannon had a prayer burden for us starting that Friday until Sunday. She didn't know about our granddaughter until Sunday, where it was announced in the service.

The Saturday after Kelly's surgery, I was scheduled to play in a church sponsored golf tournament with Rich, which I had to remove myself due to all of the events that were happening. I was really looking forward to playing and wondered how everything worked out with Rich. After Stan called me that Monday morning, I received another call from Rich, who filled me in on all of the details of the tournament. Rich also asked if there was anything they could do for us, like prepare a meal. I told him that we had plenty of food, but that I would appreciate another opportunity to play golf with believers. He said, "I will tell you what I will do. I will call you with an opportunity to play every week." Those words brought a stream of tears once again. It was as if God was concerned about even the little things. I don't think our son ever saw his dad weep so much.

Each of these events played a part in God's calling for me, which involved writing. I needed to retire, which involved getting good financial management on our investments, which Rich helped to coordinate. The men's group has been both a source of strength and an encouragement. I don't know how people handle the setbacks life throws at them without a group of people sharing a common faith as support. We can worship our Creator anywhere, but the true power of belonging to a church comes from the fellowship of its people. We cannot get that by staying in our homes. The early church was commanded to share together. They were not told to stay home and wait. Dottie and I are so thankful to our church families, which extends from New York to Florida.

On Tuesday prior to Kelly's surgery, my daughter and I met with a hospice representative in a waiting room on the floor where Dottie had been admitted. Several questions were answered that helped bring some peace to the situation. Dottie's oncologist told us that it was the right time to consider hospice and that Dottie's condition was "at the beginning of the end." Knowing whom to call when we knew she had passed away was a big question. Dialing 911 did not make sense. Having hospice meant calling them and things would be handled by them in the best interest of everyone. I felt relief after talking with the representative. A two o'clock meeting to sign up was scheduled for the following day, Wednesday.

That evening our daughter received an e-mail from a lady on her prayer chain, who had been praying for Dottie from the beginning. The e-mail stated that she had joined hospice six weeks ago. That struck a chord and our daughter immediately e-mailed her back to discuss. We scheduled a meeting an hour before the other scheduled hospice meeting at the same waiting room at the hospital. By this time we had even more questions to ask, especially those concerning the administering of IVs, should Dottie need them to avoid dehydration. Not only did she answer our questions to our satisfaction, but also she was only five miles away from our house. The other hospice was over twenty miles away.

While meeting with the second hospice, another lady was present in the room. Her brother was dying of pancreatic cancer so she was okay with the discussion about to take place. She had previously shared a portion of her conversion experience, with the highlight being thirty-two hymns that she wrote. This was amazing for several reasons. First, she could not sing, at least not like an accomplished vocalist. Second, she wrote down the words as if they were given to her by God to write down. Third, the gift of the hymns came after she asked God to come into her life and take control. Finally, she spoke the words of several of the hymns to us and we were genuinely moved. I believe God placed her in this room for a divine appointment with us.

When I received the hospice packet in the room at that time, I opened it to see the words "a legacy of love." I directed my daughter to those words and she said, "Dad, that's your book." I felt it was a sign that this was the hospice service for us to use. The lady in the room asked if I was a writer. I said that I enjoy writing, but this was a book that I wrote for my family. She asked what it was about and I shared the story of my dad, my mom, and other events. The lady said, "This is your calling from God. You must publish the book." Others before shared similar words, yet somehow this woman had credibility. Still, I thanked her and shrugged it off. The next day I brought her a signed copy to read. The thought of publishing was still only a fleeting thought. I signed with the second hospice. When the original representative came for his two o'clock meeting, I shared the news that we would be going with the other hospice.

Then came the mule-kick to my head. On Thursday it was now time to contact the hospice organization to have provisions made at our home for anticipating Dottie's release from the hospital. The hospice that we had chosen had a problem involving insurance. I had two plans. One was through my present employer, denoted as primary. The other was a secondary plan from my previous employer, which would change to my primary carrier upon retirement. The secondary plan was accepted but I would need to have the other plan sign off. This was not possible while I was still working. Therefore, I had to sign with the original hospice. "Why did my daughter get that e-mail for the second hospice?" They sounded like they offered more. They were closer to our home. Then it dawned on me that I had to meet the lady and the words *legacy of love* needed to be viewed. I was told to seek publishing and I shrugged it off like all of the other times. God desired that I tell His story. It was no longer a legacy for my family, but God wanted to use it for his.

I was awestruck. The Wednesday Bible study dealt with faith and works. The discussion further tried to define *works* as more than feeding the hungry or giving clothes to the poor. The term *works* meant allowing God to be seen in you. In other words it was a term of bearing fruit nourished by God. Was this the work God had for me? The following scripture leaped out of the page, even though I had read it many times:

> For we are God's workmanship, created in Christ Jesus to do good works, which God prepared in advance for us to do.
>
> Ephesians 2:10 (NIV)

To recognize that God preplanned my entire life for a specific purpose was beyond words to describe. I began to get more answers to questions that had long been buried like, "Why did my mother die so young?" and "Why did three boys have to endure those years without a mom?" God had a plan to reach many more people for His kingdom and used my family. God chose a Jewish mother who sought to know

Him better and accepted Christ as her Savior. If Mom had not done that, God's plan may not have been complete. We had to endure the trials and heartaches so that we would have a better understanding of God's infinite love. Even when there is no one else, we still have a loving caring God, who will not leave us or forsake us. God had a message for all of mankind that says it is never too late to come to him as long as we have breath, like my dad at eighty-nine years of age. Though we may find ourselves inadequate as a parent, God can certainly direct our paths.

What a legacy, indeed. When I knew that this is what God had planned for my life, I wept. Receiving a call from God is one thing, but my wife had to reach the point of hospice for me to realize it. Then I asked myself, "Why did I have to go to Houston?" Then I remembered the business card with the publishing book title and located it in my wallet. The coffee shop must have been in Houston, because that is the address on the front of the card. All along, God had been leading me, including the initial writing of the manuscript. Now I knew what I had to do. I started praying to the Lord about healing my wife, since I got the message. God had other plans for Dottie, but I knew what I had to do. I have since purchased the publishing book. This manuscript may be the one God wants for me to use. I will wait on Him for direction.

Ephesians 2:10 demonstrates that each of us has a purpose. Our time in this earthy world is not a mistake. First, we are God's workmanship. Workmanship is synonymous with craftsmanship and a quality product. With God as the Creator or Craftsman the end result adds an unprecedented level of perfection beyond human design. From the very beginning each of us is part of a plan that goes well beyond human understanding. When we grasp that concept, we begin to set aside our emotional questions. When we accept God's calling and purpose for our life, feelings of abandonment are replaced with an awesome joy to serve our Creator. At least that was my feeling.

Second, we are created "in Christ Jesus." A piece of furniture may be made of wood with spectacular workmanship. A painting uses a canvas to display the artist's design. We are created in Christ, who is alive, unlike the materials of canvas or wood. We will present God's workmanship by not sitting in a room or on a wall. We are living beings with the attributes of Christ Jesus.

Third, our purpose is to do good works. Museums can display priceless works of art, but people need to enter to see the workmanship. Our charge is to go out into the world and bring God's work to the world. God desires for people to see His attributes of love and forgiveness actively displayed in each of us. We are not to claim these things for ourselves and hoard them in the confines of our homes. People need to see Christ in us.

Finally, our purpose was prepared in advance for us to do. In other words we are not here by accident. Our Creator, who sees the greater picture, has carefully planned the events in our lives. We endure human emotions and hardships, but when we come to the realization that our lives are planned in advance, we can praise God through the circumstances.

When scripture comes alive our very soul leaps for joy. *Why* questions began to get answered. I began to look at my life's events with a whole new perspective. The dark glass that I was looking through became clear. The story of my family needs to be shared with the world and I have been chosen as the messenger.

PROVERBS 1: 8 - 9 (NIV)

Listen, my son to your father's instruction and do not forsake your mother's teaching. They will be a garland to grace your head and a chain to adorn your neck.

ROMANS 15: 4 (NIV)

For everything that was written in the past was written to teach us, so that through endurance and the encouragement of the scriptures we might have hope.

LESSONS TO BE LEARNED

EMOTIONS OF A MAN

My father saw comrades die before his eyes during the war and had to bury his emotions to get through each day. Soon after returning home his life took a positive turn and the stored emotions could have been placed in dormancy with the new focus on a partner and family. These emotions would rear their ugly head when everything began to fall apart. Grief in the loss of a wife was compounded with frustrations felt when family members refused to help. Financial woes further stirred the emotional caldron. Abusive foster parents, no vehicle, and barely enough income to survive would add to the restless volcano of emotions held inside him. Bitterness and anger were the symptoms that I would see or feel.

Then we can speak about Mom's cancer and how it must have created a spiritual battle within dad as well. Rae had been seeking answers to the growing spiritual emptiness she felt. I am certain that she shared her feelings with Dad before they learned of the cancer. I'm equally sure that Mom shared her feelings of relief when she truly felt that her prayers had been answered when she accepted Christ as her personal Savior. Perhaps, Dad believed that God would heal her right up until she passed. I can only imagine what he was going through in his spirit when all his hopes were dashed and she was taken away. He probably said something like, "What kind of loving God would take her away after she had made such a deep commitment to follow Him?" Then he might have thought: "How can I follow a God like that?"

The emotional unrest began to surface along with a spiritual denial in Dad's heart. For most of his life, we never knew where Dad stood in his spiritual journey. Our new mother was also Jewish, but did not actively pursue her faith. How terrible it would be if we left this world rejecting the very Creator of our being. Except for the love for his three boys, that could easily have been the case for Dad.

I believe things in our lives happen for a purpose beyond anything we can imagine. The war, the loss of his companion, and many other things could have caused him to reject God, but it did not. Perhaps, if Mom had lived and shared her spiritual experiences with Dad may have persuaded him to accept God's gift of salvation, but I will never know. I do know that his life was spared after three days in the apartment with only the faculties that he would need in tact to make a personal decision to know Christ. I can't help but think about my Lord dying and resurrecting after three days for all of us, including me. I truly believe that three boys and a dad needed an advocate in heaven to keep our lives from straying. I believe Mom's prayers reached Heaven's throne. I believe God will honor her heartfelt dying wishes to see her family again. I believe her faith in Christ was strong, despite her bout with cancer shortly after her conversion. If God was not going to heal her, then surely He would watch over her family.

All of Dad's emotions turned away from a loving God. Reading, stamp collecting, bridge playing, bowling, stamp collecting, puzzles and other mind-oriented processes filled Dad's idle times. Yet God was there with him all the time. The three days in his apartment without food, water, or medicine following his stroke could have been life ending. Instead, God removed Dad's ability to perform the tasks Dad used as an escape, like card playing, stamp collecting, and puzzle solving. Facing God was imminent. Dad's mind was in tact, which led him to the decision to accept Christ as his personal Savior and Mom's prayer was answered.

Dad held a grudge for fifty years, yet God remained faithful. As long as we have breath, we have hope. Age does not matter. Dad was eighty-nine years young.

EMOTIONS OF A CHILD

I believe that the most important time in our lives when we are shaped for the future occurs during our childhood years, especially the first five. If we are born with the ability to think, reason, and store information, then it makes equal sense that we have a somewhat empty slate of memory area to begin the process. A one-year-old can be seen actively exploring his or her new surroundings and then mimic the actions of those in his/her path. There may be some residual training that occurs in the womb, but most of what makes us who we are begins with our experiences in the world where we are placed.

What shaped my life? I appeared to be a normal happy child in the pictures taken during my first few years. I don't recall seeing any pictures of me between the years when mom died and when dad remarried. I can only imagine that my cheerfulness was replaced with doubt, fear, sadness, guilt, and frustration. When mom left I was probably feeling responsible. I may have asked thoughts or questions like:

> *What did I do to cause her to go?*
> *What can I do to get her back?*
> *I must be a bad boy.*
> *Who will help me?*
> *Doesn't anyone love me?*

Feelings can be expressed outwardly or repressed inward. As a child I believe my deepest emotions were the latter. The problem is that I did not know they were there as an adult. If I did, then I would have dealt with them.

> I would recommend that anyone who is going through life with feelings of frustration, to seek healing. I have a much deeper appreciation for those trained to recognize undesired conditions in people and help to alleviate them. The child, who felt all of those feelings of abandonment, fear, and guilt as a three year old, was still there all through my adulthood only now the screams were redirected. My wife should have been my best friend and I was pushing her away. I sincerely hope that my story helps even one person recover from events that keep them trapped emotionally.

I truly fell in love with my wife. That fact has not diminished over the years. Rather, I believe our love and respect for each other had grown. Dottie's death left a huge emptiness in my life. Whatever emotional differences were there, prior to our reunion in Georgia, had been resolved. The child in me had stopped screaming, "Doesn't anyone care."

I was empowered with more highly developed reasoning

skills than many others and it to me was a deficit. When it comes to science or math we can solve problems by applying known learned principles. We can see the results and have the confidence that they are correct. When we try to apply the laws of reason to solving emotional problems, we may also believe that the results are correct. To us they are and we may be asking a question like, "Why can't you understand?" Then when our wife (or significant other) doesn't get it we somehow think that it's because we didn't say it clear enough and we say it again. When it still doesn't get across to our satisfaction we start shouting and think it must be because we didn't speak up before. This escalating process drives huge wedges between spouses, parents and children, along with a host of other relationships. The key element for me was frustration.

- Frustration occurs when we see something as clear as day and can't seem to have others see the same things no matter how hard we try.

- Frustration occurs when children try to use all of their communication skills to get what they desire and don't get it. This is frustrating for both the child and the parent.

- Frustration in children can manifest itself with tantrums, anger, and other undesired results. The same can be said for adults.

- Frustration can lead to anger, bitterness, or resentment.

- Emotional frustration can lead to ultimate destruction like suicide along with divorce, extra-marital affairs, and sickness.

Emotional anxiety should be dealt with before it becomes frustration, anger, or something worse. I think we have been created as human beings to share our feelings with others instead of letting them burn as embers within. We have something very special that is not true for most other species. We have the ability to have relationships with others that goes far beyond animal instincts. We must seek to build positive relationships with trust, encouragement, forgiveness, empathy, understanding, and unselfishness. The relationship we have with our Creator needs to be foremost and a source of strength beyond human measure.

> I remember reading many years ago of a California college student who was writing a thesis on the effect of a breakdown between the senses of hearing and speaking. The student reasoned that we hear at a rate five times, ten times, or even higher compared to our speech. In other words, we have to reduce the rate at which we say something for it to be understood. A breakdown would be when we speak at the rate at which we hear. To test the theory a child around the age of three's voice was taped while throwing what would be considered a tantrum. No one understood what the child was saying. When they slowed the tape down to about ten percent speed, the words "red truck" were discernable. The student then went into the room and handed the child a red truck from the toy area. The child immediately calmed.

Just because we think we are communicating does not mean that we are. Stored emotions often speak an indiscernible language to others. Knowing that my heavenly father can interpret our mumbled communication is comforting. God speaks to us as well using every sense we have, especially through other people. Our life is a preplanned journey and those in our path may well be God's messengers to us.

During my wife's battle with cancer, God sent several people to minister and provide information. The communication process is not complete without discernment. When God speaks and we are open to listen, the message is delivered. Emotional relief and the joy of serving a loving God were mine, when I let God speak. Now the communication process is continuous.

EFFECTS ON BROTHERS

My brothers have experienced the same traumas as I did except at different ages. The loss of affection at three was something that I desired back from my wife. My older brother had the affection and affirmation for about four and one half years when it was taken away suddenly. I believe that it had an even harder impact on him. Douglas had less than two years to feel the love and affection of our mother. For him, the level of need for that intimacy may have been somewhat less.

Nevertheless, each of us experienced a measure of frustration, when our expectancies were not met. We often would feel something coming over us that gave us some warning of a potential blow up in the form of a raging temper. For every warning signal there was a time when we would explode unannounced. The experiences of our childhood had an impact on our emotions.

I believe that three boys placed in foster homes, where we remember many of the same abusive experiences, had the biggest impact on our emotional growth. The abandonment of a parent could have been replaced with love and affection from others to provide emotional relief. Instead we felt physical harm and were petrified of the monster in the closet. We screamed out for help and none arrived while we were still able to scream. "Isn't somebody out there who cares about us?" was, perhaps, our loudest cry. Since Dad did not have the means to visit us, due to loss of income and a car, we may have felt betrayal by our own father.

Three small boys did not know what it meant to belong and feel love after Mom passed. I must have deeply longed for the feelings of warmth and safety that existed before. My experiences had an impact on my early maturity. Perhaps the same can be said about David. Yet we knew we lacked something that we had before and desired for it to be returned. Our lives would yearn for something to hold on to that was positive and reinforcing. Our accomplishments may have given us a sense of purpose or achievement, but when we did not receive the reinforcement from others, we would question them. I believe there is a lesson for all parents today to spend time with their children and affirm them for who they are. A lack of affirmation to a child can be taken as rejection. Three brothers had felt enough of that for a lifetime.

If my brothers feel the same emotional frustration that I have described, then I would encourage them to seek for ways to get reinforcement from within. We deserve the right to tell ourselves that the things we are proud of are good things. When we place that burden upon others, we will be disappointed. Our intellectual genes were given an extra measure of potential. We could solve math problems with relative ease, but solving emotional unrest defies logic. Perhaps, this book can help even one person recognize and seek help for their emotional shortcomings. Perhaps, a marriage might be saved from divorce or a child spared abuse. Somehow, the emotional issues that plagued much of my life may serve to bring awareness to others bringing about healing.

At this point I will put my brothers aside and speak for myself. Without knowing it, I may have belittled those who did not understand my feelings or the things that I was attempting to communicate. How can I expect others to see the things I see or feel what I feel? Yet, somehow that is what I did at home, at work, or elsewhere. My thoughts would construct a picture that saw a finished product, which others couldn't possibly see. Somehow I will make them see what I see and then they will understand. Rarely does that happen and my frustration leads to negative consequences.

The measure of a person's worth is not the praise returned from others. When it is not returned frustration results, which is the catalyst for a loss of temper, anger, withdrawal, emotional disorders, or in some cases, suicide. Often the accomplishments, that may well have been very meaningful, would stop, simply because there was no one to affirm them. Unmet expectations are crushing to a person who places them above the accomplishments. When the reason for doing something is measured by the praise that will follow, then they are being done for the wrong reason. I cannot help but consider the Pharisees during Jesus' time, who sought for recognition and may have lost their own souls. Jesus called them hypocrites.

Dave and I have both been guilty of seeking gratification for something we have done, but in different degrees or categories. We both take pride in our accomplishments. I believe there is a difference between us in how we handle criticism. Dave seems to have the gift of teaching. He is very good at researching a subject thoroughly before presenting it to an audience. He does an excellent job presenting those topics that he has done his homework. As a high school science teacher, he taught about the Darwin Theory of Evolution as if it was absolute fact. A student, who believed that an omnipotent God created the earth and everything in it, would not fare well in Dave's class if he or she did not answer the test questions as they applied to Darwin.

Those times had a profound impact on Dave after he accepted Christ. The training, which he so earnestly accepted as truth, was now shattered. Dave's new faith dictated that he taught a lie for several years. To his credit he applied the same energy in finding evidence to support the theory of creation over evolution. He has applied this new knowledge to lessons on "Science versus Creation" in his local church. This accomplishment is not a small one and as his brother, I am very proud of Dave's accomplishments.

The Apostle Paul was much like that as he defended the Laws of Moses. He believed what he was doing was the right thing until the road to Damascus. There, Christ met him and blinded him for three days. When I read the account in Acts, I found it very interesting that the Lord used a light shown only around Paul to get his attention. It was as if Paul saw a clear purpose to stop the new Christian movement and he needed to see something new. Often a bright light may help us to see more clearly, but this one temporarily blinded Paul. When he regained his sight, Paul now applied the same zealousness used to defend the law, now to defend Christ. Somehow, I see my brother doing the same with his "Science versus Creation" lessons. I am equally sure that God is smiling as well. Knowing that alone should be cause for affirmation.

I wrote a book on industry practices about fifteen years ago and gave copies to many of my associates along with family. I don't recall any specific feedback from either my wife or my older brother, but a great deal from others. Doug tended to be humorous by criticizing every word on the first page, but stopped there. It is the nature of siblings to look for things that will make them look good and gloss over the accomplishments of the others. The things I might accomplish might come across to Dave as a challenge or threat to his own accomplishment. I wish I knew, while we were growing up, how to provide some level of reinforcement to my brothers for things they felt good about. I wish I could have said words of encouragement to Dave when he won his National Honor Society scholarship. I wish I understood Doug's inner feelings following his Vietnam experience and could give him comfort. Three brothers longed for acceptance in varying degrees. I think there is a lesson there for each of us to understand regarding the needs of love, acceptance, and brotherly love, especially during the early years of childrearing.

The desire for reinforcement seems to leave people with many things started and few completed without continuous gratification. The heroes of our world are those who pursued their desires and dreams despite the obstacles and through the disappointments. Hellen Keller, Beethoven, Abraham Lincoln, and many others come to mind. I have learned to set attainable goals, and then trust myself to achieve them. Often things are not achieved because people wait for everything to be perfect, which rarely occurs. I remember a phase in industry where projects apply the following steps to reach conclusion:

ASSESS . . examine where you are

PLAN. . . . design improvement actions based on assessments

DO . . . . . . perform the planned activities

VERIFY . . re-examine the results

The process looked very sound on the surface. Management embraced the concepts. Instructions were given to engineering members to start the assessing phase. Then the planning sessions would take input from each participant and it looked like the ball was now rolling and picking up steam. I can still see a long wall covered with paper representing the Assess and Plan stages. I also remember seeing only one piece of paper on the wall labeled *do* and nothing on the *verify* area.

What's my point in this illustration? Verification of a job well done comes after the task is done. Seeking gratification from others can stifle the best-laid plans. Receiving affirmation as a child can help build confidence as an adult. Losing affirmation at an early age can also build a desire to regain it with each accomplishment in life. Having affirmation replaced with abuse and the emotional trauma can handicap a person's self worth.

Thomas Edison took over three thousand attempts to perfect the light bulb. That implies that he had over three thousand less than perfect ones. We need to take risks when we feel something is worth the risks and not wait for the approval of others. I am a *doer* and my frustration comes from seeing things, which have positive potential, stagnate by indecision or lack of commitment. Who are the people that made a difference in your life? What would you like to see accomplished? Are you willing to start the process, knowing that some things may still need to be worked out?

God used Abraham, Noah, Moses, and the list goes on, to perform tasks without seeing the full picture. All of us make mistakes along the way, yet God sees the total picture and knows what will be accomplished. In other words, our role is to take the first steps independent of what others think. I spent much of my life seeking gratification from others and now desire only God's approval.

There is something good to be said about brotherly rivalries as they tend to create unique and valued differences. Children seem to seek areas where they feel a sense of belonging. My brothers developed those differences. Dave, for example, also taught himself to play a guitar, wrote songs, and entertained many people with a strong set of vocal chords. I never learned a single chord, but always enjoyed listening to his music. I remember times when we would get silly together and make up new verses, especially humorous ones. I think those times were bonding ones where encouragement was felt, although quickly forgot the next day. When my daughter dedicated her first child, she desired for Dad and his brothers to sing together for the occasion. In some ways I think it rekindled the moments when we sang around a campfire as a child. It felt good.

My younger brother, Doug, lost his world of normalcy before he reached two. His sense of awareness of what happened may not have asked the questions of guilt, but they still sensed the loss of affection. At that age a child may seek to find a replacement for some satisfaction. A common thread for each of my brothers, myself included, is that we would turn frustration into some degree or expression of anger. Our tempers would get the better of us. We would elevate our voices as if to say, "If you didn't hear me then I will speak up." As husbands this would cause further separation from our wives. As fathers we could cause the same questions to be asked in our children as we were asking, namely: "Don't you love me, Dad?" or "What did I do to cause this reaction in you, Dad?"

Unresolved emotional conflicts from childhood:

- Others are not responsible for solving our emotions. We should not place these burdens on family members. My wife was my help-mate and not my problem solver.
- Dealing with frustration or anger is our responsibility alone. We can seek professional council for help, but no one has ownership except us.
- When we feel frustrated, we need to learn to lower our voice instead of raising it. Others can sense our pain without feeling threatened.
- We need to stop crying out, "Doesn't anybody care?" and accept that our family cares very much. Best of all God cares and is always with us.
- Harmful habits or actions need to be replaced.
- We need to tell ourselves that the accomplishments we make are good even when we don't hear it from others.
- We need to be more open to hear what our wives or children are saying without muddling the issues with our own thoughts.

I desired that the negative emotions, which I had been carrying around for fifty years, be purged and replaced with the love that I lost as a child. God has been there for me all along. Philippians 4:13 says, "I can do all things through Christ who strengthens me." That was my wife's favorite verse. It was also her legacy to me. God loves us beyond measure. What better source to draw relief for our deepest emotion pain.

POWER OF PRAYER

Throughout this manuscript I have shared about having a guardian angel and relating that angel to my mother. To be more accurate, I would like to put into perspective what I now believe.

When my mother learned about her cancer and that there was no earthly cure, I believe she began a vigil of prayer. It may well have gone something like this:

> *Lord Jesus. If it is your will to remove this disease from my body, then I pray for that healing. If you have another purpose, then I welcome that plan for my life as I have placed my trust in you. I carry a burden for my new family that is great while I remain and I need your help. I pray that you would minister to David, Dennis, and Douglas, for my loss will be difficult for them to bear. Bless them Lord and send minister-*

ing spirits to guide them as they grow. Then my heart goes out to my husband as he loses even more. Keep each of them in your care and most of all; I pray that they come to know you as their loving Savior as I have.

I believe Mom left this world with a peace in her heart that went beyond human understanding, as she knew that her prayers would be answered. God had given her a desire to achieve, which took her from an orphanage to graduating from college. Perhaps she longed for a family and God answered that prayer even before she trusted Jesus as her personal Savior. I believe in an all-knowing God, who knew Mom's heart and the decisions that she would make in the future, including her search for spiritual truth. Somehow, I feel strongly that my mother had peace before she died.

The prayers of the righteous are powerful. I see Mom as devout and right with God. I believe that God honored her last wishes and sent ministering spirits or angels to guide all the members of her family. It explains how a neighbor could see through a car, see a little girl trapped in the wheel well and say exactly the right words that would save her. It further explains how an eighty-nine-year-old man, who harbored bitterness in his heart, would survive three days unconscious in his apartment alone, then come to know Christ, and feel released from his emotional bondage. The emotional trauma, which I have carried throughout my married life, has been lifted and I have been given a new purpose in life.

Never underestimate the power of fervent prayer as it intercedes for the welfare of others. My prayer for God to watch over my children if I was taken away was answered long ago. Was my heart so stirred because of the prayers of my mother over twenty years earlier? I remember praying that prayer daily until I received my answer that God was in control. I wonder if we carry the same burdens of others praying before us. Nevertheless, God doesn't measure time in days or years, as he is eternal. "With the Lord a day is like a thousand years, and a thousand years are like a day" (II Peter 3:8). I believe our prayers transcend time covering many generations.

The power of a mother's prayer was evident in my life, the lives of my brothers, and in leading Dad to a heavenly reward.

CONCLUSION

The fear of abandonment, like I must have felt after Mom died, is a powerful force. When combined with the terror of being locked in a room with a monster it can have almost irreversible consequences. For my brothers and I we felt these things in various degrees. Each of us reacted with various needs, but one of these was the need to be loved again. Measures of expectancy may have been placed on our spouses that may have been more than they should have to handle. Yet, for each of us, we owe a debt of gratitude to our wives for their support through years of emotional pressure. To my wife, I will always be grateful for just being there for me.

I believe that the most powerful emotion involves love. When we understand that people care about us, we draw from our inner supply of strength. Recognizing the source of our negative feelings is the first step to overcoming their consequences. When these feelings are mixed with absolute fear, the results can cause even deeper emotional scars long after the things we fear are removed. I would like to think that this document would help even one person cope with their emotional monsters. That is one of the reasons that I have for writing. I now understand the reasons for my negative emotions and that's the first step for positive change.

I also desire for those who read this to take from it the knowledge that we are not in this battle alone. I believe that we have an enemy out there who will devour us if we let him. I further believe that we have a loving father in Jesus Christ, who has already defeated our enemy. For those who have lost a parent early in life, there is hope in knowing that we have a replacement that loves us even more. I will not know why Mom had to leave when I was three until I see Jesus and ask, but I have been given a glimpse of the joy that I felt in dad's salvation.

For those, who have worked their entire life for recognition, know that the recognition from our Creator is far better than that of man. People will let us down even when they are not aware of it, because the expectations are not theirs. God will never let us down. He was there for our earthly father even when, Dad denied Him. The lives of those we love should not be under so much pressure to perform that the relationships are strained to a breaking point. Like our mother's legacy, when she put herself through college as an orphan, the joy of completion should be our joy. When we get to Heaven we can have eternity to view our stored treasures.

For those struggling with inner turmoil, you can have true peace in your life. The same kind of peace that I believe both our parents had before their deaths. Raging emotions need to be dealt with before they cause personal destruction or harm to others. The emotions felt by three brothers in the loss of a mother could have caused negative repercussions, like failed marriages, but God sent people to help us through the difficult times. The mental and physical abuse from foster homes may well have delivered lasting scars, but God provided healing with families to be proud of.

The last two years of my wife's life brought emotional closure between us. God surrounded us with a peace that seemed to say everything was all right. Our devotion to each other and our family was unquestionable. Dottie was selfless and demonstrated that quality to all who knew her. I can imagine the words of Jesus saying, "Well done my child. Well done."

Finally, I leave this as a legacy to my son, Jeff, and daughter, Tricia. Mom and I are proud of you both. You may not have understood some of the things caused by Dad's emotional conflicts, but rest assured you are deeply loved. My thoughts, feelings, hopes, and dreams will always be for you to achieve whatever is your heart's desire. Who knows what prayers Mom left this world uttering in her heart? Rest assured, God heard them, and is still working in your lives. To your children will flow immeasurable blessings. Enjoy!